# LEAD & MANAGE

# Lead & Manage

## BRIDGING THE GAP TO DEVELOP YOUR UNIQUE LEADERSHIP IDENTITY

Shawn Eaton

# Contents

| | | |
|---|---|---|
| Dedication | | 1 |
| Introduction | | 2 |
| **1** | Introduction to Leadership | 6 |
| **2** | The 11 Principles of Leadership | 13 |
| **3** | How to Communicate | 26 |
| **4** | Building and Leading Teams | 33 |
| **5** | Decision Making and Problem Solving | 41 |
| **6** | Leading Change | 47 |
| **7** | Emotional Intelligence in Leadership | 55 |
| **8** | Developing Leadership Presence | 61 |
| **9** | Difference between Leadership and Management! | 68 |
| **10** | Functions of Management | 77 |
| The Key Differences And A Thanks | | 95 |

*About The Author*     97
*Bibliography*     99

# Dedication

This book is lovingly dedicated to two remarkable women who have shaped my understanding of leadership through their actions and influence: my mother and my wife.

To my mother, thank you for embodying the essence of perseverance and discipline. Your dedication to hard work has not only provided for our family but has also set a stellar example of what one can achieve with the right focus. I am deeply grateful for the countless hours you spent ensuring we always had enough, a testament to your boundless love and care.

To my cherished wife, Randi, your unwavering support has been my anchor for 18 years. Through numerous deployments and life's uncertainties, you have been the cornerstone of our life together. I cannot thank you enough for keeping me grounded and for being the heart of our home. Your presence makes every day brighter and our journey together richer. Thank you for always being there.

# Introduction

Writing this book came as a culmination of a globe-trotting adventure in leadership, seasoned with over two decades of distinguished service in the United States Army. Picture this: a young soldier, turned sage through myriad encounters with the crème de la crème (and occasionally the crème de la crap) of Army leadership.

Rewind to the start, where leadership wasn't about medals or ranks, but about a superhero without a cape—my mom. She juggled a demanding job, five kids, and an endless list of chores with the dexterity of a circus acrobat, instilling in us the values of hard work and resilience. Meanwhile, my father, a Navy Senior Chief Petty Officer, unfortunately, showcased the type of leadership that was a masterclass in what not to do. His idea of discipline was as misplaced as a penguin in the Sahara, teaching me early on the profound impact of leadership styles.

From these contrasting examples sprouted my intrigue in leadership dynamics. Life took a turn, and I found myself in Arkansas, under the wing of my mom's boyfriend-turned-stepdad, a man whose leadership style was akin to Yoda—less about scolding and more about guiding. His mentorship, although it chafed at the time, was the scaffold upon which my understanding of positive influence and correction was built.

With a heart full of dreams and slightly naive bravery, I enlisted in the Army, aiming to be a 19K-Armor Crewman. In my mind, a tank was the ultimate iron fortress—until reality checked in. The Army unfolded as a kaleidoscope of leadership: the good, the bad, the ugly, and the extraordinary. I recall a Drill Sergeant who, contrary to the stereotypical hard ass, believed in shining boots and shooting hoops, teaching us excellence and teamwork, albeit with a side of tough love.

My career was an exhilarating rollercoaster, packed with deployments that spanned continents—from the deserts of Iraq and Afghanistan to the historical landscapes of Europe. I found myself in leadership roles for the majority of my service, a journey of self-discovery and evolution.

Initially, I mimicked the only style I knew—loud and forceful, a reflection of my earlier influences. However, I quickly realized that leadership was not a one-size-fits-all. Witnessing the spectrum of leadership in the Army, from the shouty sergeants to the more composed higher-ups, was enlightening. It dawned on me that true leadership was less about echoing the past and more about carving a path that encourages growth, unity, and respect.

To my astonishment, there came a day at the office (and by the office, I mean the kind where the scent of gun oil beats out the aroma of coffee) when my Soldiers found themselves on the receiving end of a cleaning spree. Not the spring-cleaning type, but the "Platoon Sergeant thinks our weapons could be cleaner than a Michelin-star kitchen" type. Armed with my vast, almost legendary, leadership prowess, I did what any self-respecting leader would do: I channeled my inner drill sergeant, complete with a symphony of yells and a sprinkle of colorful language. After all, nothing says "motivation" quite like the threat of impending doom—or so I thought.

Just as I was about to award myself the "Sergeant of the Year" award for my impeccable leadership style, another Platoon Sergeant called out to me. And not in the "I'm going to scare you into next week" kind of way, but more of a "Hey, you, with the vocal cords of steel, over here" kind of yell. Intrigued and slightly less ferocious, I made my way to his office. The conversation that ensued wasn't just a wake-up call; it was the whole alarm clock factory going off.

"Why," he inquired, "do you accept as true with that the most effective manner to speak together along with your Soldiers is thru the historic artwork of shouting and belittlement?" To be fair, I hadn't taken into consideration my technique as belittlement a lot as motivational speaker for the difficult of hearing. However, it was evident that my troops might have received a different message.

The next quarter of an hour didn't just adjust my leadership compass—it completely recalibrated it. He posed a question that hit me harder than a morning PT session: "Have you ever considered, I don't know, just asking your men nicely?" That query did not simply open my eyes; it almost carried out LASIK surgical operation on my expertise of leadership. Fast forward 27 years, and that moment is as fresh in my mind as the day it happened. It was like discovering a new flavor of leadership that wasn't just effective but also didn't leave everyone involved with a need for throat lozenges.

With this groundbreaking concept in mind, I awaited my golden opportunity. It presented itself when my driver, in a moment of human forgetfulness, left something in our tank. Instead of deploying my previously preferred method of vocal persuasion, I simply asked him if he could retrieve it. His response? A calm and collected "No problem, Sergeant." It was a small exchange, but the impact was monumental.

This revelation didn't just change my approach; it even had the peanut gallery whispering. "Are you getting soft?" chuckled a fellow NCO. To which I replied, "Just trying out a new battle strategy." Even my Platoon Sergeant chimed in with a nod of approval, unaware of the seismic shift that had occurred in my leadership philosophy.

When my Soldier returned, not only did he complete the task, but he also offered a "No problem, sergeant, I got you!" That response was more rewarding than any "HOOAH" I had ever elicited through sheer volume. It was then I realized the true power of dignity, respect, and, dare I say, a more serene form of command.

This anecdote underscores a trio of leadership pillars I hold dear: perpetual improvement, the golden rule of treating others as you wish to be treated, and the understanding that there's more than one way to lead effectively.

This book isn't just a collection of my musings on leadership, but I also added the point of managing versus leading. This a guide is designed to lay a solid foundation for good leadership, peppered with both my escapades and those of leaders I admire. My aim? To offer you insights that not only enhance your leadership style but also equip you with the tools to mentor effectively and have a full understanding of managing. So, as you turn these pages, I hope you find both inspiration and practical advice that resonates with your journey toward becoming a leader worth following.

Let's kick things off with a dive into the ever-elusive world of "leadership"—what it is, what it's not, and why it occasionally enjoys playing hide and seek with us. Then, we'll tango with its close cousin, "management," a term that's both exhilarating and terrifying, like deciding to organize your sock drawer at 2 AM. By the time we close the cover on this literary adventure, you'll not only have mastered the textbook definitions of these two powerhouses but also gotten a front-row seat to the rollercoaster of anecdotes and real-life shenanigans that have seasoned my own voyage through the treacherous but often hilarious realm of adulting.

# 1

# Introduction to Leadership

Leadership, a multifaceted skill that lies at the heart of all successful endeavors, bridges the gap between aspiration and achievement. This chapter delves into the essence of leadership, its critical importance, and the characteristics and styles that define effective leaders.

**What is Leadership?**

At its core, "leadership" is the art of motivating a group of people to act towards achieving a common goal. In a short sense, it is about providing purpose, direction, and motivation. Yet, a deeper exploration reveals leadership as the ability to influence, inspire, and guide others towards a shared vision. It encompasses qualities such as vision, integrity, empathy, decisiveness, and adaptability. Leadership can manifest across various domains, from professional environments and community organizations to personal relationships. The hallmark of effective leadership is not just in achieving results but also in empowering and nurturing the development of team members, promoting innovation, collaboration, and positive change.

Just as the captain of a football team or the lead of a cheer squad takes on the responsibility of inspiring their team, guiding them forward, and accepting the outcomes of their collective efforts, it seems like a heavy load for just one individual to bear. Yet, it's a journey filled with numerous silent steps that bring their teams closer to their goals.

Similarly, a Sergeant instructs their soldiers on what needs to be done, how it should be executed, and the reasons behind the actions. But does this necessitate a harsh or commanding tone? Is it required to delve into every minute detail? Does it imply there's only a single pathway to achieve the objectives? Or perhaps it means...

**Why is Leadership so important?**

Ah, the grand enigma of leadership—why on earth does it matter? Well, strap in, because leadership isn't just a buzzword your overly caffeinated CEO throws around; it's the secret sauce that can either make or break the world's greatest teams, organizations, and, occasionally, garage bands. Here's the scoop on why leadership is the MVP of the professional world:

Think of leaders as the captains of the SS Enterprise (yes, a "Star Trek" reference—we're professionals, not dead inside). They're here to navigate through the cosmic void of business challenges, armed with nothing but a star map and a can-do attitude, pointing everyone towards the treasures of success.

Leaders are the ones turning the office into a place where dreams don't go to die. They light fires under people (figuratively, please), getting everyone jazzed about Monday mornings and spreadsheets.

Behind the curtain, leaders are pulling levers and pushing buttons, making tough calls, and solving problems with a blend of magic and logic, ensuring the show goes on, despite flying monkeys.

Imagine your team as a bunch of succulents—low maintenance but still needing some TLC. Leaders are the green-thumbed enthusiasts ensuring everyone gets just the right amount of sunlight and tough love to blossom.

Leaders are the folks asking, "But what if we made it edible?"—pushing the boundaries of what's possible, encouraging a culture where ideas bloom like wildflowers (and yes, some are just weeds in disguise).

They're crafting a workplace vibe that's more "cool startup" and less "dreaded family reunion." Leaders use their powers for good, shaping spaces where respect, empowerment, and really good coffee reign supreme.

Good leaders are like that super-strong adhesive you used once and accidentally glued yourself to a table. They build trust and collaboration so well; teams stick together through thick and thin (without the need for emergency services).

At the end of the day, leadership is all about crossing that finish line, preferably without anyone on fire (metaphorically or literally). It's about steering the ship to new horizons and celebrating those wins, big or small.

What makes a leader stand out? Is it the cape? The ability to look good in corporate headshots? Let's decode the DNA of leadership greatness:

*The Decider:* Quick to call shots, leaders are like those friends who actually decide where to eat out.

*Moral Compasses:* With integrity as their North Star, they navigate the murky waters of ethics without turning into pirates.

*Trust Fall Champions:* They catch you when you fall—because they've built a trampoline of trust and reliability.

*Humble Pie Eaters:* Even leaders need to dine on a slice of humble pie, serving their team with a side of support.

*Confidence Conjurers:* Their belief in the mission is contagious, and suddenly, you're infected with optimism.

*Bravery Buffs:* They say "Yes" to risk the excitement of a toddler in a candy store, embracing failure like an old friend.

*Influence Infusers:* They don't just lead; they inspire you to follow, crafting a vision so compelling you'd follow it on social media.

*Empathy Engineers:* They get you. Really, they do, making the office feel less like a gladiator arena and more like a supportive group hug.

*Dream Weavers:* With a vision as clear as a 4K TV, leaders paint a picture of the future so vivid, you'll want to live there.

*Action Heroes:* Always in the thick of it, leaders are more hands-on than a toddler with finger paint, driving the team forward with energy and enthusiasm.

*Cheers Squad:* Recognizing your wins, leaders are the first to give a standing ovation (even if it's just for successfully refilling the printer).

The United States Army's definition of Leadership is short, straight forward and to the point: *"The process of influencing. people by providing purpose, direction, and motivation while operating to. accomplish the mission and improve the organization."*

**Leadership: The Genre Spectrum**

Leadership styles are like movie genres—there's something for everyone, but not all will be your cup of tea:

- **Autocratic** Action Flicks: Where one hero calls the shots, and the explosions (or decisions) are big, bold, and unilateral.
- **Bureaucratic** Documentaries: Rules, regulations, and more rules, with a side of paperwork.
- **Democratic** Dramedies: Everyone gets a say, and the results can be as heartwarming as they are productive.
- **Laissez-faire** Indies: Freedom reigns supreme, where creativity and self-direction are the stars of the show.
- **Participative** Musicals: Everyone's voice matters, leading to harmonious decisions and the occasional show tune.

Leadership isn't a one-size-fits-all hat; it's more of a versatile accessory that shifts with the times, teams, and goals. By mixing and matching these styles, effective leaders become the maestros of their orchestras, creating symphonies of success that resonate far beyond the office walls. Now, who said leadership had to be dull?

To better give understanding of this chapter, here is a real example utilizing the information contained in Chapter! I call this story "Silent Night".

### *Silent Night*

*Deep in the mountains of Afghanistan, where the whispers of the past mingled with the echoes of today, a young Lieutenant, Second Lieutenant (2Lt.) Sialana led one of his squads with command and control, with vigor and excitement, with confidence and bravery yet all of which aroused both awe and loyalty throughout the squad. Their mission was clear, yet frightening! They were to navigate through the mountains well within the enemy lines undetected and use the darkness as cover and patrol to a nearby village then at sunup meet with the town leader and conduct a secret KLE. (Key Leader Engagement).*

*It seemed like the night had no moon, the darkness so dark that there was no ambient light to be found, the night vision goggles were almost useless, and all the tree cover didn't help. Sialana's squad still moved diligently and with confidence as if it was bright as day throughout the mountain. The lieutenant's squad, a tapestry of courage woven from the diverse threads of humanity, moved silently, each step a testament to their trust in Sialana's leadership as they ventured through the unknown.*

*Aware of the price and cost at hand, 2lt. Sialana had thoroughly planned every detail that he could think of for the operation. With the understanding that leadership isn't about being a tough guy or a measurement of manhood; it is about embodying the confidence and clarity that his squad required to navigate the uncertainties of war!*

Nearing the village, only about a football field away, still under concealment from trees and the dark, the mission was about to get very interesting! Standing between Sialana's squad and the village was a large gathering of men. 2Lt Sialana couldn't see any weapons but out of caution, he motioned to his platoon to take a knee. As the team froze and took a knee, their mission now hanging by a thread, one of the Soldiers saw a silhouette of the men and confirmed they were carrying weapons. 2lt Sialana, being cool calm, and collected, displayed such confidence, even though inside his chest his heartbeat was faster than drumsticks doing a drum roll, he motioned for Sergeant First Class (SFC) Dell, his second-in-command, to come to his position as SFC Dell happened to closer to the enemy so going to Sialana's location was a wiser decision. Sialana knew that together they would need to craft some kind of diversion. Understanding that leaders must be aware of their capabilities and ask for help when needed Sialana requested Dell because he had been in combat numerous times before. Sialana wanted Dell's input on the decision-making more now than ever.

They knew that time was running out, but they still had to make the KLE and get back to the Combat Outpost (COP) before the sun came up, SFC Dell and 2lt Sialana knew they had to act quickly. Developing a plan and quietly distributing it throughout the squad, their strategy was simple yet bold. The plan was to throw a flash grenade away from their location so it could create a loud noise but also in a safe location where it couldn't hurt anyone. This would create enough chaos that it would give his platoon a window to bypass the insurgence and enter the village safely. Trusting in the lieutenant's leadership, the squad executed the plan flawlessly. The diversion created just enough of a diversion that the squad was able to slip past the gathering of men and reach the village.

Not having a Quick Reaction Force (QRF) available and with strict orders to remain undetected as this was to be a secret meeting, Sialana and Dell knew they had to find an alternate route back to the COP. The mission was *a delicate dance of precision and timing. Sialana directed his squad to move under complete darkness, secure a perimeter, communicate silently with hand signals, and lead the charge into the heart of the village. The Afghan village leaders, fearing the worst as they too heard the noise, were met instead with the determined faces of Sialana and his team.*

*The return journey was fraught with danger, but Sialana's unwavering leadership guided them back to safety. His ability to adapt to unexpected challenges, to inspire and direct his squad through the darkest of nights, was a testament to the importance of leadership.*

*Back at the COP, the team debriefed, and the impact of 2Lt Sialana's leadership was clear. It was not just the success of the mission that marked this as a victory, but how it was achieved. Sialana had led not with an iron fist, but with a heart of courage and a mind sharp with strategy.*

Ultimately, the narrative of that night transformed into a profound illustration of leadership's influence. Lieutenant Sialana and the squad encountered formidable challenges, yet it was their leadership that crafted a narrative not dominated by conflict but highlighted by hope, cohesion, and the indomitable nature of the human spirit.

The Silent Night transcended its initial designation as a mere mission; it emerged as a testament to the idea that within the vortex of turmoil, the light of leadership possesses the strength to illuminate the path back to safety and solidarity. This episode serves as an enduring reminder that even in moments of profound uncertainty and disorder, effective leadership can foster a sense of direction, unity, and resilience.

# 2

# The 11 Principles of Leadership

Leadership isn't just herding cats or juggling flaming torches in a stiff office breeze; oh no, it's more like conducting an orchestra where the instruments are people's wills, skills, and aspirations. It's about striking a chord between the "do, know, and be" - transforming them into a symphony of actionable insights that don't just manage but lead with pizzazz. This chapter is your backstage pass into the world of leadership, diving into the eleven commandments (well, principles, but who's counting?) that elevate mere mortals to maestros of motivation.

As we pull back the curtain, prepare to embark on a journey of self-discovery, tuning your leadership skills to the key of "effective," with a minor in ethics and a major in values. It's about learning to lead not just with your brain and brawn but with your heart, guiding your team through the thick and thin with the grace of a gazelle and the wisdom of an owl. So, sharpen your pencils (or styluses), and let's decode the enigma of leadership together, ensuring you're well-versed in the art of inspiring, innovating, and, occasionally, improvising.

1. Know Yourself and Seek Self-Improvement: Keep Growing The foundation of effective leadership lies in self-awareness and the relentless pursuit of self-improvement. Leaders who are committed to their personal growth continually seek knowledge through books, courses, and other educational means. This constant learning process not only enhances their leadership skills but also inspires their teams to follow suit. By embodying the principle of lifelong learning, leaders position themselves to navigate the complexities of their roles with greater ease and effectiveness.
2. Be Technically Proficient: Know Your Stuff Technical proficiency in one's field is essential for earning and maintaining the respect of one's team. A deep understanding of the job, along with a comprehensive grasp of the team's functions, establishes a leader's credibility. This credibility is crucial for guiding the team effectively, making informed decisions, and fostering a culture of respect and excellence.
3. Seek and Take Responsibility Leadership involves taking initiative and assuming responsibility for the organization's direction, successes, and failures. By embracing responsibility, leaders demonstrate commitment and accountability, inspiring their teams to adopt the same values. This proactive approach is vital for driving organizational growth and achieving long-term success.

**Decision-Making and Communication**

1. Make Sound and Timely Decisions The ability to make informed, timely decisions is a hallmark of effective leadership. Utilizing problem-solving and planning tools can aid leaders in navigating decision-making processes efficiently, ensuring that decisions are both sound and expedient.
2. Keep Your People Informed Communication is a cornerstone of leadership. Keeping team members informed about goals, processes, and changes is essential for ensuring alignment and

fostering an environment of transparency and trust. Effective communication bridges the gap between leadership and the team, facilitating a cohesive and motivated workforce.

**Developing and Empowering Others**

1. Develop Responsibility in Your Team Leaders have the responsibility to nurture character traits in their team members that empower them to execute their responsibilities with integrity. This development is crucial for building a reliable and ethical team capable of meeting its objectives.
2. Ensure Tasks are Understood and Accomplished Clear communication and oversight are key to ensuring that tasks are understood and executed effectively. Leaders must ensure that team members have a clear understanding of their responsibilities and the standards to which they are held.
3. Train Your Team A cohesive, efficient team is built through deliberate development and team-building activities. Investing in the team's growth not only enhances its capabilities but also strengthens the bonds between team members, contributing to a more effective and unified group.

**Utilizing and Maximizing Resources**

1. Leverage the Full Capabilities of Your Organization Fostering a team spirit and leveraging the collective resources and talents of the organization are crucial for maximizing efficiency and productivity. Leaders who effectively harness these resources can drive their teams to achieve greater outcomes.
2. Set the Example Leadership by example is a powerful tool for influencing the behavior and work ethic of a team. Demonstrating the qualities and dedication expected from team members motivates them to embody these traits in their work.

3. Know Your Employees and Look Out for Their Well-Being
Genuine concern for the well-being of team members builds trust and loyalty, which are essential for a productive and positive work environment. Leaders who prioritize their team's well-being not only enhance morale but also encourage a stronger commitment to the organization's goals.

**Understanding Self as a Leader**

Embarking on the journey to understand oneself as a leader is akin to going on a self-discovery safari, armed with nothing but a flashlight and a notebook, deep into the jungle of your own psyche. It's about digging deep into your leadership toolbox to figure out which tools you actually know how to use and which ones you've been using as paperweights. This expedition requires a hefty dose of introspection and reflection, almost like meditating, but instead of reaching enlightenment, you're trying to figure out why your team looks terrified every time you say, "I have a great idea."

As you navigate through the dense underbrush of your strengths, weaknesses, values, beliefs, and the ever-elusive impact these have on your ability to not just lead but inspire, you start to piece together the leadership mosaic that is uniquely yours. It's about understanding that your leadership style might be less of a well-oiled machine and more of a quirky Rube Goldberg contraption that somehow gets the job done. *(Rube Goldberg was an American cartoonist, sculptor, author, engineer, and inventor. Goldberg is best known for his popular cartoons depicting complicated gadgets performing simple tasks in indirect, convoluted ways.)*

This self-exploratory voyage isn't just about patting yourself on the back for every time you didn't cause a team mutiny; it's also about facing the music when it comes to your decision-making symphony—identifying whether you're more of a smooth jazz leader or a death metal dictator when it comes to steering the ship and dealing with your crew.

In essence, grasping the reins of self-awareness as a leader is about discovering how your unique blend of traits orchestrates the harmony or chaos within your team. It's a professional and humor-filled quest to become not just a boss, but a maestro of leadership, directing an ensemble where every member plays their part in perfect pitch.

## Evaluating Strengths and Weaknesses

*Cultivating Self-Awareness:* At the heart of leadership lies the serene journey of self-awareness. It is here that leaders embark on a reflective path, acknowledging their emotions, recognizing their strengths and vulnerabilities, and understanding the values that steer their course. This process is integral, not only for personal growth but also for enhancing interactions within the team. It's about gently uncovering one's emotional landscape and recognizing how these inner currents influence the waves made in professional relationships.

*Embracing Values and Ethics in Leadership*: The essence of leadership is profoundly rooted in ethics and core values. It's like a gentle stream that nourishes the soil of trust, guiding decisions with a compass of integrity and shaping the organizational culture into a haven of positive influence. This commitment to ethical leadership serves as a beacon, not just resolving conflicts with grace but also ensuring that the organization's endeavors cast ripples that benefit society at large. It's a reminder that at the leadership helm, holding steadfast to one's ethical beliefs illuminates the path for others, crafting a legacy of trust and respect.

## The Guiding Lights of Work Life: Values and Ethics

Picture yourself as an adventurer in the sprawling corporate wilderness. Here, your values act as a personal compass, navigating you through challenges, helping choose your path at life's crossroads, and cautioning you when you're on the brink of a figurative cliff.

Ethics, akin to a meticulously crafted map, draw on the collective wisdom and standards of society to guide you through unknown terrains, ensuring you remain the hero in your professional saga, rather than a cautionary tale in someone else's.

**Values: Your Personal Guiding Star**

Values are incredibly personal, akin to a friend who navigates by the stars on a cloudy night. They underpin what matters most to us, mold our beliefs, and shape our actions. In the workplace, these values determine whether we aim to change the world, seek fortune, or daringly try to achieve both, holding onto the hope that these goals are not diametrically opposed.

Imagine your values as a whimsical compass: at times, directing you with confidence towards altruistic acts, like supporting a colleague, and at other moments, driving you to perfect an email for hours, all in the name of "excellence." This internal compass is what makes you uniquely you, guiding every decision from ethical considerations to choosing eco-friendly office supplies.

**Ethics: The Roadmap with Detailed Guidelines**

Ethics represent the moral principles shared by a community or society, functioning like a universal map that outlines the do's and don'ts. In the realm of work, ethics govern how businesses operate, ensuring fairness and transparency in all dealings. They provide the framework for tackling complex issues, from accountability in mistakes to balancing profit with environmental care.

Adhering to ethical standards can feel like navigating a complex game with philosophical rules—complex, sometimes conflicting, but always crucial. These guidelines are the bedrock of trust, respect, and integrity in the workplace, safeguarding our professional journey from misdirection or, even worse, detrimental errors.

## Values and Ethics: Navigating the Professional Voyage Together

Values and ethics together form the powerhouse that steers us through our careers. They inspire us to be the protagonist of our own story rather than the antagonist in someone else's. While values offer personal direction, ethics provide the collective guidelines ensuring our journey is both honorable and fulfilling.

Grasping and aligning our personal values with broader ethical standards transforms us not just into better professionals, but into better individuals. As we journey through the professional landscape, let's ensure our compass is calibrated and our map current. Echoing the sage advice of philosopher-comedian Jon Stewart, truly held values are not mere hobbies; they are tested and true beacons guiding us through life's grand adventure.

Trust and Credibility are ethical behaviors that earn respect and trust, also essential for effective leadership.

*Decision-making* is huge as its values provide a moral compass for making complex decisions.

*Culture and Influence* can make a difference in the retainability rate. Leaders shape organizational culture through their ethical actions and values.

*Sustainability and Success* are the focus shifts toward fostering long-term viability and prosperity in leadership roles, teams, and organizations through sustainable practices. This concept is multi-faceted, incorporating the endurance and growth of leadership impact over time, ensuring that success is achieved without compromising the future. Ethical leadership correlates with long-term organizational success and sustainability.

Having the ability to use *Conflict Resolution* is a skill that evolves daily. Ethical leaders effectively manage conflicts, maintaining team cohesion which results in mission accomplishment.

Leaders must ensure their organizations positively impact society and the environment. *Societal Responsibility* is a positive light on the organization.

Leadership, at its core, reflects one's character and values. It requires a deep understanding of oneself, a commitment to personal and professional development, and a dedication to ethical principles. By adhering to these principles, leaders not only inspire and empower those around them but also leave a lasting impact on their organizations and communities.

## Crafting Your Leadership Development Plan (PLDP)

A Personal Leadership Development Plan (PLDP) stands as a vital tool in this journey, offering a structured and strategic approach to enhancing one's leadership capabilities. This chapter delves into the creation of a PLDP, guiding you through identifying your leadership goals, assessing your current skills, formulating development strategies, and setting an action plan for growth.

### Identification of Leadership Goals

*Long-term Vision:* Embarking on the leadership journey begins with envisioning the kind of leader you aspire to become. This vision might encompass attaining certain leadership roles, embodying distinguished leadership qualities, or initiating transformative changes within an organization or community. It's about setting a horizon to strive towards—a compelling picture of your future self in a leadership capacity.

*Short-term Objectives:* To bridge the gap between your current state and your long-term vision, setting short-term objectives is crucial. These objectives are immediate milestones that pave the way for your overarching goals. They could involve acquiring new leadership skills, enhancing your emotional intelligence, or taking on specific roles that expand your experience.

**Self-Assessment:** A critical introspection into your existing strengths and areas for development forms the foundation of your PLDP. Utilizing tools such as personality assessments, leadership style inventories, and skill assessments can provide valuable insights into your leadership profile.

*Feedback from Others:* The perception of your leadership by peers, subordinates, and mentors offers an external perspective on your effectiveness. Engaging in 360-degree feedback mechanisms facilitates a comprehensive view, highlighting areas of excellence and opportunities for growth.

*Skill Development:* Identifying and targeting specific leadership skills for development is key. Whether it's enhancing your strategic thinking, mastering conflict resolution, or improving your public speaking abilities, pinpointing these skills provides a focused direction for your growth.

*Experiential Learning:* Real-world leadership experiences contribute significantly to your development. This may involve leading a project, volunteering for new initiatives, or assuming a mentorship role—each experience enriching your leadership journey.

*Formal Education:* Engaging in formal education through workshops, seminars, and courses equips you with the theoretical and practical knowledge necessary for leadership. Pursuing relevant certifications can also bolster your leadership credentials.

### Personal Development Activities

### Expanding Your Horizons: The Unofficial Guide

Broadening your perspectives isn't just a nice-to-have; it's the secret sauce in your professional development stew. Think of activities like devouring leadership books, schmoozing with fellow trailblazers, or getting peace with mindfulness as a gym membership for your leadership muscles. They're about as vital to your growth as coffee is to your Monday morning.

**Action Plan: Your Roadmap to Awesomeness**

You wouldn't set off on a treasure hunt without a map, so why approach your development goals any differently? Sketch out those steps, complete with deadlines and "X marks the spot" milestones. This isn't just about having a plan; it's about making sure your plan doesn't end up as just another pretty document gathering digital dust.

Time, money, support—these are the currencies of your quest. Pinpoint what you'll need to bankroll this adventure because let's face it, even the most ambitious plans can flop without the right backing. Think of it as packing your survival kit before heading into the wilderness.

How will you know you're getting closer to your treasure? Self-check-ins, constructive criticism from your crew, or hitting specific targets are your compass. Keep tabs on your journey so you can do more of what works and toss what doesn't overboard.

Just like you periodically check your phone for updates (admit it, you do), regularly review your progress. This isn't just navel-gazing; it's about assessing what's paying off and what's a sunk cost. It's about fine-tuning your strategy for maximum impact.

The only constant in life is change, and your Personal Leadership Development Plan (PLDP) should be as adaptable as your choice of coffee depending on the time of day. New experiences, feedback, and shifting goals aren't just hurdles; they're opportunities to recalibrate your course.

A PLDP isn't just another item on your to-do list; it's your dynamic blueprint for not just growing as a leader but becoming the kind of leader who leaves a mark. By putting in the time to craft and adapt your PLDP, you're not just setting yourself up for success; you're laying the groundwork for a legacy of influence. So, arm yourself with this living strategy, and prepare to make your leadership journey not only intentional but legendary. Next is a short story of a Non-Commissioned Officer and his leadership journey.

## *The Lead with the Led*

*Sergeant (Sgt) Jesse James stood before a group of Soldiers. James was an Army instructor, and this was his first rotation as such. He was a bit nervous because these Soldiers were recruits. The recruits all come from varied backgrounds, and some are pretty rough. He noticed that these recruits started with the wrong impression of the Army. James didn't know what they had exactly experienced but he wasn't going to let that thought stick in their head. These recruits had a bad taste in their mouths, but James didn't think that mattered.*

*Sgt James loves the Army, has an unwavering commitment, and is dedicated to making the Army a career. As James identified the challenges in his near future, he looked at the glass half full instead of the glass half empty.*

*Sgt James has a pretty good grip on what kind of leader he is and how he wants to be. He is proficient and has a strong understanding of the 11 Principles of Leadership. James has always considered these principles the foundation of leadership and led with those in mind. Having faith in the principles, Sgt James committed to applying them in his leadership style every day. James had to overcome the challenges of changing the negative thoughts of the Army that these recruits had developed. Knowing he has a great opportunity to show these recruits what right looks like and James hopes to change how they feel about the Army, he took full advantage of the opportunity.*

*Fast forward a couple of weeks of training James has demonstrated being technically proficient, and he continuously sought self-improvement. It was important to James that the recruits had an opportunity to discuss opportunities for improvement with him. The recruits noticed their sergeant taking the time to conduct a self-study and seeking feedback! James also worked hard to understand the recruits' strengths and weaknesses, and this didn't go unnoticed. It became a secret discussion among the recruits. James felt he needed to lead this way to be more effective and provide the best training he could.*

As part of any great team, Sgt James believed communication was key to success when developing a team. James made a point of keeping his recruits informed of their progress and the expectations from higher-ups. He wanted to make sure everyone was on the same sheet of music. He worked on developing their responsibility, ensuring tasks were clear and achievable, and fostering a team spirit that leveraged the full capabilities of the group.

Setting the example and leading from the front has been drilled into his soul since he was a young private. Sgt James spent a lot of time ensuring that the wellbeing of his recruits was attended. He built trust and loyalty with them and enhanced their morale and productivity too. Sgt James is such a humble leader that he even decided to share his own Personal Leadership Development Plan (PLDP), highlighting the continuous journey of leadership with his recruits.

The moment of truth! It's time to operate as a team and be evaluated on their performance. The recruits, once boisterous and divided, now operated as a cohesive unit, embodying the principles they had been taught. Their success was a testament to their hard work and James's leadership.

The recruits performed and met the standards. Exceeding some standards. Sgt James decided he should reflect on this journey. The application of the eleven principles not only transformed his recruits but also deepened his understanding of leadership. He realized that leadership was not about authority but about inspiring and empowering others to achieve their best.

James could only hope that he had a positive impact on his recruits. His influence extended far beyond the training, but it molded every recruit. Changing the minds of his recruits was one of the biggest obstacles he would overcome. His recruits would continue and implement the leadership they learned from watching Sgt James. For James, the journey was far from over, but he took pride in knowing he had laid a foundation of leadership.

The last thing Sergeant James said to his recruits before he released them to their Units was, "Always remember, the lead with the lead!" One recruit *asked what that meant, Sgt James with a smirk on his face, I was once the "led" and now I'm the lead. Lead from the front and never forget where you come from!*

Through Sergeant James' journey, the story summarizes the core of the eleven principles of leadership, proving how they can guide effective leadership and foster personal and professional development, both for the leader and those they lead. James' story is a testament to the transformative power of leadership that is rooted in self-awareness, commitment to ethical principles, and a dedication to empowering others.

# 3

# How to Communicate

**Communication Skills for Leaders**

Effective communication is the linchpin of leadership. Whether it's guiding teams, executing strategies, or nurturing relationships, the ability to communicate clearly and listen actively underpins all facets of leadership. This chapter unfolds the essence of communication for leaders, exploring effective communication strategies, active listening techniques, and the art of giving and receiving feedback.

**Effective Communication Strategies**

Imagine you're a modern-day Romeo but in the digital era, but instead of a balcony, you've got social media, texting, and the occasional coffee shop encounter. The quest? To communicate with Juliet—not with lutes or sonnets, but with the suave sophistication of a leader in the art of modern chit-chat. Here's your cheat sheet, infused with a dash of humor and a pinch of charm, for navigating the labyrinth of love communication today. Oh, and these are also great pointers to communicate as a leader. I just wanted to make it a funnier read!

The Staring Contest (Maintain eye contact with whom you are speaking with): Think of eye contact not as a creepy, unblinking stare but like your WiFi connection but to her soul! It's strong, uninterrupted, and full of bars—signaling that you're fully logged in and ready to engage!

The Feedback Loop-de-loop (Request and receive feedback): Cultivate a garden were feedback blossoms like wildflowers. You toss a compliment her way, she shares a thought, and together you cultivate a vibrant ecosystem of growth. Just remember, feedback is like a boomerang—it should always come back.

The Sacred Art of Zipping It (Don't interrupt): Your mission involves mastering the ancient technique of keeping thy mouth shut when needed. Interrupting her is like hitting pause during her favorite song or part of the movie—you're a goner! Listen more and watch your conversation playlist hit all the right notes.

Distraction Demolition (Limit distractions): In the realm of heartfelt gab, distractions are the dragon you must slay. Put your phone on silent, banish pop-up thoughts of your fantasy football team, and give her the spotlight. It's like turning off notifications in your brain to update later.

Laser-Focused Listening (Focus on what the other person is saying): Engage with her words as if they're the last pieces of chocolate in the world (Hope you like chocolate). Savor them, appreciate them, and let her know you're all in. It shows you value her thoughts more than the finale of your favorite series.

Tone Tuning (Focus on your tone of voice): Your voice isn't just an audio output; it's a mixtape of your emotions. Play it right, and she'll hear the sincerity in your Spotify playlist. Wrong tone? You might end up on her blocked list.

The Pen is Mightier (Good written communication): In a land dominated by emojis and LOLs, be the one who knows the power of well-crafted words. Texts and DMs are your scrolls—make them clear, make them witty, and for the love of autocorrect, make sure they make sense!

The Silent Symphony (Good Nonverbal Communication): Master the orchestra of nonverbal cues. A nod here, a smile there, and a posture that says, "I'm open to this symphony of conversation." It's like playing charades where everyone wins.

Epic Listening Quests (Active listening techniques): Activate your listening ears with the skill of a legendary hero. It's not just about catching her words; it's about understanding the quest she's on. Nod wisely, ask questions that show you're on the journey with her, and resist the urge to solve her puzzles unless asked.

Silence is Golden (Using Body Language): Sometimes, the most powerful message is delivered in the quiet between words. It's the pause that says, "I'm thinking about what you've just shared," not, "I've fallen asleep with my eyes open."

Feedback Feasts (Asking and giving Feedback): Feast on the banquet of feedback, a delicacy that enriches both giver and receiver. It's like Yelp for conversation—helpful, constructive, and designed to make the next visit even better.

Armed with this information, you're ready to step into the arena of romance (leading) with the confidence of a CEO stepping into the boardroom. Just remember, the goal isn't just to win the game; it's to co-create a storyline filled with laughter, mutual growth, and a connection that could give any broadband a run for its money.

**Guidelines for Giving Feedback Successfully**

- Jump in Early: Tackle challenges head-on to avoid letting them balloon into bigger problems.
- Mind Your Motives: When offering feedback, aim to uplift and assist, rather than pick apart.
- Collaborate on Feedback: View feedback as a team sport where everyone works together to score solutions.
- Double-Check for Clarity: Make sure everyone's on the same page by clarifying and welcoming new insights.

- Keep Cool: Focus on the matter at hand, keeping personal feelings in check to maintain a clear course.
- Celebrate Variety: Embrace the rich tapestry of different viewpoints and methodologies.
- How to Ace Receiving Feedback:
- Be Feedback Hungry: Regular feedback is the secret sauce to personal and professional development.
- Embrace Feedback: Keep an open heart and mind, and welcome feedback as a gesture of goodwill.
- Tune in Fully: Listen with the intent to truly grasp the feedback, not just to formulate a comeback.
- Dive into the Discussion: Share your views and explore pathways to betterment together.
- Say Thanks: Show appreciation for the time and effort invested in giving you feedback.

Mastering the art of communication isn't just about talking the talk; it's about walking the walk with empathy, insight, and a readiness to grow. By weaving together effective communication tactics, fine-tuning your listening skills, and navigating the seas of feedback with grace, leaders can cultivate an environment rich in trust, respect, and collective striving towards greatness.

Here is a quick story that illustrates the transformative power of effective communication in leadership. Through Dave's journey, you will gain insights into practical strategies for enhancing their communication skills, the significance of active listening, and the delicate art of giving and receiving feedback. As we see in Dave's experience, these skills are not just the linchpin of leadership but the foundation of meaningful, collaborative relationships.

### *The New Leader*

Dave stepped into their new role with a mixture of excitement and anxiety. Tasked with steering a diverse and talented team through an ambitious project, they quickly realized that technical prowess alone wouldn't suffice. Early on, a pivotal meeting underscored the importance of non-verbal cues and tone. When presenting their strategy, Dave's avoidance of eye contact and a hesitant tone inadvertently sowed doubt among the team. Feedback from a mentor illuminated this misstep, highlighting how eye contact and a confident tone could bolster credibility and foster trust.

### The Power of Listening

Determined to improve, Dave embraced the challenge head-on. They meticulously prepared for the next team meeting, focusing not just on what to say, but how to say it. The transformation was unmistakable. By maintaining eye contact and adopting a firm yet encouraging tone, Dave's message resonated, instilling confidence, and sparking a lively, productive discussion.

However, another lesson awaited. An overeager Dave, in their enthusiasm, frequently interrupted team members, unknowingly stifling valuable input. A one-on-one with a quiet but insightful team member revealed this flaw. The conversation, marked by Dave's intentional silence and attentive listening, unveiled innovative ideas that had been simmering beneath the surface. This epiphany underscored the importance of not just speaking well but listening even better.

### Fostering Open Communication

Emboldened by their newfound understanding, Dave adopted active listening techniques. They made a conscious effort to fully engage with speakers, employing body language and questions to demonstrate interest and understanding. This shift had a remarkable effect. Team meetings became more dynamic, with members feeling genuinely heard and valued. The exchange of *feedback, once a source of anxiety, transformed into a constructive dialogue that propelled the team forward.*

### Mastering Feedback

*The art of feedback presented its own challenges. Initially, Dave's attempts at providing constructive criticism were met with defensiveness and discomfort. However, by applying the principles of timely, intention-driven feedback, Dave learned to frame their insights as opportunities for growth. They encouraged dialogue, ensuring that feedback was a two-way street. This approach not only diffused tension but fostered a culture of mutual respect and continuous improvement.*

*Similarly, receiving feedback became an exercise in humility and growth. By actively seeking and graciously accepting feedback, Dave not only enhanced their own leadership skills but also set a powerful example for the team. The willingness to listen, adapt, and improve inspired the team to adopt a similar mindset.*

### The Transformation

*As the project neared completion, the team reflected on their journey. The contrast between their initial struggles and their ultimate success was stark. Through Dave's leadership, they had not just achieved their goals but had grown closer, more collaborative, and more resilient. Dave's commitment to effective communication, active listening, and meaningful feedback had transformed the team's dynamics, fostering an environment of openness, trust, and mutual respect.*

In the end, Dave realized that their greatest achievement wasn't the project's success, but the lessons learned along the way. Leadership, they discovered, was less about directing and more about connecting, less about speaking and more about listening. By mastering the art of communication, they had not only led their team to victory but had also embarked on a lifelong journey of personal and professional growth.

# 4

# Building and Leading Teams

The essence of effective leadership lies not only in the vision one holds but significantly in the ability to build and guide a team toward realizing that vision. This chapter explores the foundational elements necessary for nurturing positive team dynamics and development, crucial for a team's performance, creativity, and overall satisfaction.

**Clear Purpose and Goals**

Think of a shared vision as the team's group chat - where everyone's in on the plan and pumped about the group project (minus the eye rolls). This isn't just about agreeing to show up; it's about everyone getting psyched to build the next big thing, like crafting the world's most epic sandwich together. That unity? It's the secret sauce that turns a bunch of individuals into a dream team, ready to conquer the world (or at least the boardroom).

The Treasure Map: Setting specific goals is like handing out treasure maps to your team. Each map doesn't just say "X marks the spot"; it outlines the adventure to get there, from braving the stormy seas to outsmarting the riddles in the cave. These aren't just any old maps; they're personalized, motivational, and clear enough to make Indiana Jones envious. And when does everyone's maps align? You're not just hunting for treasure; you're on a quest for greatness, with every team member a crucial part of the legend.

**Roles and Responsibilities**

Imagine if your team was a band, and clarity meant everyone knew whether they were on drums, guitar, vocals, or that fancy triangle thing. This isn't just about avoiding a cacophony of confused jamming; it's about ensuring each band member rocks their part, contributing to the ultimate chart-topper. When everyone's in tune with their role and responsibilities, the band vibes stronger, creating a sense of unity and a hit single in the making (or at least a killer presentation).

Aligning roles to everyone's superpowers (and areas for growth) is like casting for a superhero team where everyone's unique ability perfectly complements the mission. It's not about shoehorning the Hulk into a delicate negotiation or asking Spider-Man to handle the flying. Instead, it's about ensuring that each team member's strengths are spotlighted, making the team an unstoppable force of efficiency and satisfaction. This strategic casting means everyone gets to save the day *in their own way, making the workplace not just a job, but a league of extraordinary satisfaction.*

**Communication**

Picture your team as a jazz club where openness is the theme of the night. Everyone gets their turn at the mic—whether it's with a soulful ballad or an electrifying sax solo—knowing they're in a space where honesty, respect, and a bit of improv are always welcomed. This isn't just about avoiding feedback screeches; it's about making sure every voice adds to the harmony, proving that every team member is a headliner in the making.

In the symphony of teamwork, making sure you're all tuning into the same station is key. It's about picking the radio frequency that comes in loud and clear, whether it's emails for the formal notes, instant messaging for the quick back-and-forth, or video calls to bring the band back together. Selecting the right communication tools is like being the team's DJ—dropping the beat that keeps everyone grooving in sync, ensuring the workflow never misses a beat.

### Trust and Respect: The Secret Sauce for Team Awesome

Trust isn't just a nice-to-have; it's the secret ingredient in the world-class recipe for team success. Picture it as the super glue holding your team together, crafted through the magical arts of being dependable, consistent, and making sure everyone feels like their emotional safety goggles are always on.

Think of mutual respect as the spice rack of your team. Everyone's unique flavor (aka perspective) not only gets a spot on the shelf but is crucial to the gourmet dish you're cooking up together. Valuing every shake and sprinkle of individual expertise turns your team into a Michelin-star-worthy ensemble.

### Collaboration and Participation: The Teamwork Dance

Ensuring every team member can belt out their tune is key. It's like making sure every band member, from the lead singer to the triangle player, feels like a rock star. This vibe creates a platinum record of inclusion and value.

When everyone's unique powers combine, you get more than just a team; you get Voltron (*Voltron is a Transformer reference, I might be aging myself here*). Encouraging a mixtape of collaboration means the sum of your chart-toppers will outshine any solo hit.

### Conflict Resolution: Turning Battles into Brainstorms

Believe it or not, conflict is your secret lab for cooking up innovation. Handled with care, it transforms from kryptonite into a superpower, pushing your team towards groundbreaking discoveries.

*Resolution Skills*: Arming your team with ninja-level conflict resolution skills ensures any squabbles turn into opportunities for growth, keeping the team vibe positive and productive.

*Accountability*: Riding into battle with clear expectations and a banner of responsibility means everyone knows what they're fighting for. Promoting a knights-of-the-round-table level of collective accountability keeps your team in tight formation.

### Continuous Improvement: The Quest for Team Perfection

Regular feedback is the spell book for personal and team growth, a tome of knowledge that highlights both the epic quests completed and the dragons yet to be slain.

Encouraging a culture of constant learning and skill acquisition is like turning your team into RPG characters, where every new experience and training session boosts your stats for the next big adventure.

### Supportive Leadership: The Captain's Log for Navigating Team Seas

Imagine leadership as a chameleon, skillfully changing colors to blend with the scenery of team dynamics and individual quirks. This mastery of style-shifting provides the compass and map needed to sail through stormy challenges and treasure hunts alike.

Handing over the wheel doesn't just empower your team; it turns them into confident captains of their own mini ships. Trusting their navigational skills fosters a fleet of autonomy and engagement, sailing in formation towards the horizon of success.

Spotting and shining a spotlight on the gold coins of achievement isn't just nice; it's essential for keeping morale buoyant. Celebrating every island discovered and storm weathered boosts motivation like a favorable wind, reminding everyone that their efforts are the real treasures.

**Adaptability: The Shape-Shifting Ship**

Building your ship with the elastic planks of flexibility and adaptability ensures it can stretch to meet the waves of change, rather than splinter. This resilience keeps the team's compass needle steady, aimed at goals no matter how the sea shifts.

Building and leading effective teams requires a deliberate and strategic approach, focusing on these foundational elements. By cultivating positive dynamics and continuous development, leaders can forge high-performing teams capable of overcoming obstacles and achieving their objectives, thereby translating collective effort into collective success.

A compelling narrative would be to tell the story of Maya, a new CEO tasked with revitalizing a struggling company. Her journey will illustrate the application of these principles in turning around the company's fortunes by focusing on building a cohesive, high-performing team. This story will unfold in several key chapters, highlighting each foundational element mentioned in Chapter 4.

### *A Vision for the Future*

*Maya stood before her new team, sensing the mix of skepticism and curiosity in their eyes. The company, once a leader in its industry, had been floundering, plagued by poor communication, unclear goals, and dwindling team morale. Maya's first address focused on her vision for the company—a vision of resurgence and innovation. She spoke of shared goals and the importance* of a unified direction, setting the stage for a collective effort towards turning the company around.

With the vision set, Maya began the meticulous work of aligning the team towards common objectives. She initiated collaborative goal-setting sessions, ensuring that each team member could see how their efforts contributed to the larger mission. Clear, achievable goals were established, providing both direction and motivation, as team members began to see their place in the company's future success.

Recognizing the mismatch between some team members' roles and their strengths, Maya embarked on a reorganization. She met with individuals, seeking to understand their passions, strengths, and career aspirations. By realigning roles to fit these strengths, Maya not only maximized efficiency but also reignited a sense of purpose and belonging among the team.

Maya knew that trust and respect were the bedrock of a high-performing team. She led by example, being transparent about challenges and open to feedback. Team meetings became forums for honest conversation, where diverse perspectives were not only welcomed but valued. This environment of mutual respect and trust began to transform the team's dynamics, fostering a sense of unity and shared commitment.

With the team's foundation solidifying, Maya introduced initiatives to boost collaboration. Team-building retreats, collaborative projects, and cross-functional teams encouraged interaction and leveraged individual strengths in a synergistic manner. The team learned to appreciate each other's abilities, working together more effectively than they had thought possible.

Conflict, when it arose, was approached as an opportunity for growth. Maya facilitated conflict resolution workshops, equipping her team with the skills to address disagreements constructively. These skills were put to the test during a major project, where differing opinions on the approach threatened to derail progress. Through effective communication and negotiation, the team *found a solution that was better than any individual proposal, exemplifying the innovation that can emerge from constructive conflict.*

*As the team began to operate more cohesively, Maya introduced mechanisms for accountability and continuous improvement. Regular performance reviews, coupled with open feedback sessions, helped identify both achievements and areas for development. Maya emphasized collective accountability, celebrating team successes, and addressing challenges together, which strengthened the sense of community and shared purpose.*

*Empowering her team to take initiative became Maya's focus as the company started to regain its competitive edge. Delegating responsibilities, she trusted her team's decision-making capabilities, which not only accelerated progress but also boosted team morale and engagement. As the market evolved, Maya encouraged adaptability, leading her team to pivot strategies, when necessary, always with an eye on the long-term vision.*

*A year into Maya's leadership, the company had not only returned to profitability but was also innovating in ways it never had before. The team's transformation was evident at the annual celebration, where Maya highlighted individual and collective achievements. The event was not just a celebration of financial success but of the journey the team had taken together, embodying the essence of effective leadership and teamwork.*

*As Maya looked to the future, she saw a team capable of facing any challenge. The principles of clear purpose, mutual respect, effective communication, and continuous improvement had become ingrained in the company's culture. Maya's story had become one of transformation, not only of a company but of its people, who had grown stronger, more cohesive, and more resilient under her leadership.*

Through Maya's story, we see the practical application of leadership and team-building principles in overcoming challenges and achieving success. Her journey highlights the importance of a shared vision, aligned goals, effective communication, trust, collaboration, and continuous improvement in forging a high-performing team. This narrative serves as a testament to the power of effective leadership in translating collective effort into collective success.

# 5

# Decision Making and Problem Solving

In the realm of leadership, decision-making, and problem-solving are pivotal skills that steer teams and organizations through challenges toward achieving their goals. This chapter delves into the core models and techniques that facilitate effective decision-making and problem-solving, as well as handling ambiguity and risk.

Effective decision-making is rooted in structured models that guide leaders through the complexity of choices and outcomes. This model emphasizes a systematic approach to decision-making, characterized by:

- Defining the Problem: Clearly articulate the issue at hand.
- Identifying Decision Criteria: Determine what's important for making the decision.
- Weighting the Criteria: Prioritize each criterion based on its importance.
- Generating Alternatives: List all possible solutions.
- Evaluating the Alternatives: Assess each alternative against the criteria.
- Choosing the Best Alternative: Select the solution that best fits the criteria.

- Implementing the Decision: Put the selected answer into action.
- Monitoring and Evaluating the Decision: Review the outcome to ensure effectiveness.

## DMAIC Process

*DMAIC stands for Define, Measure, Analyze, Improve, and Control. It's a data-driven quality strategy used to improve processes. DMAIC is a tool of Six Sigma, a methodology aimed at lowering defects and improving the quality of manufacturing and business processes.*

DMAIC offers a structured, iterative approach to problem-solving, especially useful in process improvement:

- Define: Outline the problem, goals, and customer requirements.
- Measure: Collect data to understand the current state and quantify the issue.
- Analyze: Investigate the data to find root causes of inefficiencies.
- Improve: Develop and implement solutions to the identified problems.
- Control: Ensure the improvements are maintained over time.

## Problem-Solving Techniques

Diverse techniques provide leaders with tools to approach and resolve issues creatively and effectively. Let's go over some now:

*Brainstorming:* A method to generate a wide array of ideas, promoting creativity and participation without judgment.

*The five Whys:* A easy method geared toward drilling right all the way down to the foundation reason of a trouble through asking "Why?" repeatedly.

*Root Cause Analysis (RCA):* This approach identifies the underlying reasons for a problem, often employing tools like the Fishbone Diagram for deeper analysis.

*SWOT Analysis:* A strategic method to assess internal and external factors affecting decisions, identifying **S**trengths, **W**eaknesses, **O**pportunities, and **T**hreats.

*Handling Ambiguity and Risk:* Navigating uncertainty and risk is inherent in decision-making and problem-solving. Effective strategies include:

- *Embrace a Learning Mindset:* View challenges as opportunities to learn, grow, and innovate.
- *Increase Flexibility and Adaptability:* Be prepared to adjust plans as new information and situations arise.
- *Improve Information Gathering:* Enhance decision-making by seeking out more comprehensive and accurate information.
- *Use Scenario Planning:* Anticipate possible futures to better prepare for uncertainties.
- Implement Risk Management Strategies: Identify, assess, and prioritize risks to mitigate potential impacts.
- *Practice Decision-Making Under Uncertainty:* Develop skills to make informed decisions even when outcomes are not fully predictable.
- *Develop Resilience and Psychological Safety:* Foster a team environment where members feel secure to take risks and share ideas.
- *Foster Creativity and Innovation:* Encourage novel approaches and solutions to complex problems.
- *Use Probabilistic Thinking:* Consider the likelihood of various outcomes to make better-informed decisions.
- *Cultivate Emotional Intelligence:* Manage emotions effectively to navigate the stresses and pressures of decision-making.

Mastering decision-making and problem-solving skills is crucial for leaders to guide their teams through complex landscapes, adapt to changing circumstances, and achieve sustained success. This chapter provides the foundation for developing these essential leadership capabilities, emphasizing the importance of structured approaches, creative techniques, and resilience in the face of uncertainty.

Time for another Story. Does it seem like it's a break from reading yet? This story of Erika, a seasoned leader at the helm of NextGen Solutions, unfolds. Erika's journey through navigating her team through a critical pivot in their business model encapsulates the essence of effective decision-making and problem-solving in leadership.

## Leading NextGen through the Winds of Change

*Erika faced a pivotal moment at NextGen Solutions. The market was shifting, and customer needs were growing faster than ever. Recognizing the need for change, Erika convened her leadership team to define the problem: How could NextGen adapt its offerings to remain at the forefront of the tech industry?*

*Employing the Rational Decision-Making Model, Erika led her team through a structured process. They identified critical decision criteria, including market demand, technological feasibility, and alignment with NextGen's core competencies. After weighing these criteria, the team generated alternative strategies, from diversification to focusing on niche markets.*

*To refine their strategy, Erika introduced the DMAIC process. They defined specific goals for the pivot, measured current capabilities against market needs, and analyzed their findings to identify gaps and opportunities. The improvement phase saw the development of a new product line, while the control phase ensured the sustainability of this pivot.*

*Understanding the importance of creative input, Erika facilitated brainstorming sessions that welcomed all ideas, fostering an environment of innovation. The 5 Whys technique helped the team drill down to the core market shifts driving the need for change, while Root Cause Analysis unveiled internal processes that needed retooling.*

A SWOT Analysis provided a comprehensive view of NextGen's position, revealing strengths to leverage, weaknesses to address, opportunities to seize, and threats to mitigate. This strategic assessment informed the final decision-making, guiding the selection of a bold, new direction for the company.

With the future course set, Erika and her team faced the challenge of implementation amidst uncertainty. Erika promoted a learning mindset, encouraging her team to view upcoming challenges as opportunities. Flexibility and adaptability became their mantras, as they remained open to adjusting their strategies in response to new information.

Anticipating potential risks, Erika led her team in scenario planning exercises, preparing for various outcomes. Probabilistic thinking helped in assessing the likelihood of these scenarios, enabling better-prepared responses. Through effective risk management, they prioritized actions to mitigate the most critical risks.

As they embarked on implementing the pivot, Erika faced decisions that required judgment under uncertainty. She balanced data-driven insights with intuitive judgment, making informed choices even when full information was lacking. Her emotional intelligence guided her in managing the team's anxieties and expectations during this transformative period.

Recognizing the need for ongoing innovation, Erika fostered a culture that valued creativity and experimentation. By establishing psychological safety, she ensured that her team felt secure in proposing novel solutions, taking calculated risks, and learning from failures.

Months later, NextGen Solutions emerged as a leader in its new market domain. Erika's leadership through the pivot not only transformed the company's product line but also its culture. The team had become more cohesive, agile, and resilient, equipped to face future challenges with confidence.

Through Erika's story, we see the practical application of decision-making models and problem-solving techniques in a real-world scenario. Her journey highlights the importance of structured approaches, creativity, and resilience in navigating the complexities of leadership and organizational change. This narrative serves as a testament to the power of strategic decision-making and problem-solving in steering teams and organizations toward sustained success amidst the uncertainties of the business world.

# 6

# Leading Change

Leading change is one of the most challenging yet rewarding aspects of leadership. It involves guiding individuals, teams, and organizations through transitions to achieve lasting improvements. This chapter explores the principles of change management, strategies for overcoming resistance to change, and the steps for implementing change successfully.

**Understanding Change Management**

Change control is a complete area that specializes in preparing, supporting, and assisting people, teams, and groups in making organizational change. It combines insights from psychology, sociology, business administration, and economics to manage the change process effectively. Key concepts may include:

- Kotter's 8-Step Process for Leading Change (*Kotter's 8-Step Process for Leading Change was developed by Dr. John Kotter, a professor at Harvard Business School and a well-respected authority on leadership and change.*): A strategic framework that emphasizes the importance of urgency, building a guiding coalition, forming a

strategic vision, communicating the vision, removing obstacles, creating short-term wins, consolidating gains, and anchoring new approaches in the culture.
- Lewin's Change Management Model (*Lewin's Change Management Model, developed by psychologist Kurt Lewin in the 1940s, is a foundational concept in the field of organizational change.*): This model describes change as a three-stage process of unfreezing, changing, and refreezing, emphasizing the need to prepare for change, execute it, and then solidify it as the new norm.
- ADKAR Model (*The ADKAR Model is a change management framework developed by Prosci, a renowned change management consultancy and learning center. Introduced by Jeff Hiatt, the founder of Prosci, in 2003, the ADKAR Model is an acronym that stands for Awareness, Desire, Knowledge, Ability, and Reinforcement.*): A goal-oriented change management model that focuses on the stages of Awareness, Desire, Knowledge, Ability, and Reinforcement to support individuals through change.
- McKinsey 7-S Framework (*Developed in the late 1970s by consultants Robert H. Waterman Jr., Tom Peters, and Julien Phillips with McKinsey & Company*): A tool that examines organizational effectiveness and changes through seven interdependent elements: strategy, structure, systems, shared values, skills, style, and staff.
- Bridges' Transition Model (*Bridges' Transition Model, developed by William Bridges in the 1970s, is a psychological framework that differentiates between change and transition, emphasizing the internal journey that individuals undergo during change.*): A model that distinguishes between change (the external event) and transition (the internal psychological process people go through to come to terms with the new situation).

## The Fine Art of Herding Cats: Navigating the Whirlwind of Change

Have you seen those videos of cats disliking water. They bite and claw their way out of taking a bath or swim. It just looks painful! That's Change! It is like trying to convince a cat to take a bath. You know it's for the best, but the cat? Not so much. Here's a slightly humorous, yet instructively brilliant (if I say so myself) guide on how to not only toss that cat in the water but also make it enjoy the swim. Or, at the very least, not claw your eyes out in the process.

**The Magic Formula for De-Cattifying Change Resistance**

In the complex ecosystem of organizational change, resistance often emerges as naturally as a cat might resist a bath. Understanding and mitigating this resistance can greatly enhance the success of any new initiatives within a company. Here is an exploration of effective strategies that can be likened to a magic formula for "de-cattifying" change resistance, making transitions smoother and more accepted by all stakeholders.

When implementing change, the first step is to involve the people affected by it. This involves more than just informing them; it means actively engaging them in the decision-making process. When employees feel that they have a say in the changes, they are more likely to embrace them rather than resist. This approach cultivates a sense of ownership among team members. Like holding the soap during a cat bath, when people feel they are part of the process, they are more likely to cuddle up to the idea of change instead of hissing at it.

Transparency is another critical element. Clear communication about the reasons behind changes, how they will be implemented, and their expected outcomes can prevent misunderstanding and distrust. Just as a cat might be more cooperative if it understands a bath will involve warm water and bubbles rather than a threatening dunk, employees are less likely to resist when they have a clear understanding of the change process. Transparent communication reduces fears and allows for better preparation.

Preparation involves equipping the team with necessary skills and knowledge to handle new challenges—much like preparing to handle a slippery, wet cat. Training and development sessions can empower employees, reduce anxiety about new processes, and diminish resistance. Knowledgeable employees are more confident, and confident employees are more likely to engage positively with change.

Addressing the emotional aspect of change is crucial. Changes can stir up a range of emotions, from fear and anxiety to excitement. Providing emotional support through these times can transform a scaredy cat into a brave lion. Managers should be prepared to offer encouragement and empathy, acting as a comforting presence during uncertain times. This support can alleviate the emotional turmoil that might otherwise exacerbate resistance.

Approaching change incrementally can also help in managing resistance. Just as you would gradually introduce a cat to water, introducing changes slowly can make the process less intimidating. Starting with minor adjustments before implementing major ones allows individuals to acclimate to the new environment gradually. This method can reduce the shock and discomfort that often accompanies significant change.

Promoting a flexible and resilient mindset is another strategy that can reduce resistance. When people view change as an opportunity for growth rather than a threat, they are more likely to engage with it constructively. This mindset can be encouraged through training that focuses on adaptability and resilience, equipping employees to handle future changes more effectively, just as a cat gradually becomes less fearful of water with each bath.

Finally, individual concerns must be addressed thoughtfully and directly. Each employee may have unique worries about how changes will affect their role or personal circumstances. Addressing these concerns individually can help smooth out the metaphorical fur, ensuring that each team member feels heard and valued.

In conclusion, effectively managing change in an organization involves a combination of strategies that can be likened to the steps one might take to bathe a resistant cat. By creating a sense of ownership, maintaining transparency, equipping employees with the necessary skills, providing emotional support, implementing changes gradually, encouraging a resilient mindset, and addressing individual concerns, leaders can reduce resistance and facilitate a smoother transition. This "magic formula" not only makes the process less stressful for everyone involved but also enhances the overall success of organizational change.

### *Executing the Great Bath Plan*

Successfully guiding a cat through a bath without a trip to the emergency room is an intricate dance of strategy, preparation, and adjustment, not unlike leading a team through organizational change. Here's how this can be done, drawing an amusing yet insightful parallel to the processes involved in both situations.

Plotting the course: The first step in the process is to clearly articulate the plan for change. Just as you would explain to a cat the benefits of a bath, making it as appealing as belly rubs, so must you spell out the reasons and goals for organizational change. Clarifying the 'why' behind the change helps everyone understand its importance and aligns their expectations with the desired outcome.

Sketching the Battle Plan: Preparation is crucial. Determining who needs to be involved, what resources will be required, and the timeline for the change is akin to deciding who holds the cat, the type of shampoo to use, and how the cat will be dried. These details can make or break the success of both a cat bath and organizational change.

Engaging the Feline Council: Communication is key. Just as involving a cat in the bathing process might prevent a flood, keeping employees informed and soliciting their feedback can prevent misunderstandings and resistance. This step ensures that those affected by the change have a voice in the process, increasing their engagement and buy-in.

Initiate the Bath: Start small. Testing the waters with a kitten reflects the principle of starting change on a small scale. This allows for adjustments based on initial reactions and ensures that everyone is equipped with their 'rubber duckies'—the support structures necessary to handle the change.

Keep an Eye on the Water Temperature (Monitor and Adjust): Just as one would use a bath thermometer to ensure the water isn't too hot or too cold for a cat, so must leaders monitor the progress of change and make necessary adjustments. Using metrics to measure the impact of change allows leaders to respond to challenges proactively and keep the process moving smoothly.

Post-Bath Reflections: After the bath, it's time to reflect. Reviewing what went well and what didn't—what made the cat purr and what made it yowl—provides valuable lessons for future initiatives. This reflection phase is essential to understand the effectiveness of the change and how it can be improved in subsequent efforts.

Rub in the Catnip (Reinforce the Change): Finally, reinforcing the change is crucial. Just as a cat might be rewarded with catnip after a bath, so should employees be recognized for their efforts in embracing change. This reinforcement helps solidify the change as the new norm within the organization.

Here we go again, story time!! Now, consider Lieutenant Colonel Natalie Crawford, in the desert, addressing her battalion about embracing the integration of drones, transitioning from traditional methods to cutting-edge technology. This scenario mirrors the cat bath analogy, highlighting the challenges and strategies involved in leading change. Whether in a military operation or a corporate setting, the principles of strategy, empathy, and humor are vital. They ease the transition, foster acceptance, and lead teams through the turbulent waters of change, just as one might navigate the tricky waters of a cat bath.

### *The Call for Change*

*The need for change was undeniable. With the evolving landscape of modern warfare, reliance on conventional reconnaissance methods was no longer sufficient. Lt. Col. Crawford recognized that integrating drone technology* was not just an improvement but a necessity. Drawing on Kotter's 8-Step Process, she began by creating a sense of urgency, illustrating to her team the stark realities of the battlefield and the undeniable advantages of drone reconnaissance.

Understanding the importance of collective effort, Crawford formed a guiding coalition of officers and enlisted personnel who were either tech-savvy or showed an openness to change. This team became the champions of transformation, embodying the bridge between the old and the new.

Crawford, alongside her coalition, crafted a strategic vision: a battalion that could execute missions with unprecedented precision and safety, minimizing risks to personnel. This vision was communicated clearly and compellingly, resonating with the core values of every soldier - safety, efficiency, and the unwavering pursuit of excellence.

Resistance came from various quarters - skepticism over the reliability of drone technology, apprehension about the learning curve, and a deeply ingrained adherence to traditional reconnaissance methods. Employing Lewin's Change Management Model, Crawford initiated the unfreezing stage by encouraging open discussions, addressing concerns, and showcasing the success of drone operations in other units.

The transition phase was marked by intensive training programs. Utilizing the ADKAR Model, Crawford ensured that awareness led to desire, knowledge, ability, and finally, reinforcement. Through simulations and real-world exercises, the battalion gradually built confidence in using drones, appreciating their value in operational planning and execution.

Recognizing the importance of short-term wins, Crawford orchestrated a series of controlled missions that utilized drone technology. These early successes, minor yet significant, served as tangible proof of the benefits, boosting morale and solidifying trust in the new methodology. Each success was celebrated, reinforcing the change, and paving the way for full integration.

*The refreezing stage involved consolidating gains and embedding the new approaches into the battalion's culture. Crawford leveraged the McKinsey 7-S Framework to align the organization's elements with the change, ensuring that the new technology and methods became as foundational as the rifles they carried.*

*Despite the progress, challenges persisted. Technical glitches, logistical hurdles, and operational setbacks tested the battalion's resolve. Yet, through flexible leadership and the unwavering support of her coalition, Crawford navigated these challenges, adapting strategies as needed and maintaining the focus on the overarching vision.*

*Months into the implementation, the battalion conducted a large-scale operation that would serve as the ultimate test of their transformation. The drones provided real-time intelligence that allowed for dynamic decision-making, avoiding ambushes and pinpointing targets with precision. The operation was a resounding success, a testament to the effectiveness of the change.*

*In the aftermath, Crawford led a comprehensive review of the transformation process. Through this, the battalion identified strengths, acknowledged weaknesses, and documented lessons learned, ensuring that the knowledge gained from this experience would benefit future operations and transformations.*

Lt. Col. Crawford' leadership through this period of transformation became a case study in effective change management within the military. Her balanced approach, combining strategic planning with empathetic execution, not only steered her battalion through the challenges of change but also prepared them for a future where adaptability, innovation, and resilience were paramount.

# 7

# Emotional Intelligence in Leadership

Emotional intelligence (EI) is a cornerstone of effective leadership, encompassing the ability to understand and manage one's own emotions and those of others. This chapter delves into the significance of emotional intelligence in leadership, exploring its components, impact, and strategies for development.

Emotional Intelligence in Leadership: EI in leadership is about leveraging emotional awareness and control to inspire, guide, and achieve organizational success. It enhances leaders' abilities to navigate stress, communicate effectively, empathize with others, and resolve conflicts—fundamental competencies for successful leadership.

*Components of Emotional Intelligence in Leadership*

Leaders who exhibit high self-awareness possess a clear understanding of their own emotions, strengths, and weaknesses, and recognize how these personal attributes affect those around them. This deep self-knowledge fosters a sense of authenticity and instills confidence in their decision-making processes, allowing them to lead with assurance and credibility.

Such leaders also excel in managing their emotions, responding to situations with deliberate thoughtfulness rather than impulsiveness. By adhering to their core values and maintaining integrity, even under pressure, they uphold a standard of leadership that commands respect and trust.

Intrinsic motivation is another hallmark of effective leadership. Driven by a deep-seated passion and perseverance, these leaders approach goals with vigor and determination. Their optimistic outlook becomes contagious, inspiring, and motivating their teams, particularly during challenging times.

Empathetic leaders genuinely understand and consider the emotions of others, creating an inclusive and nurturing environment that allows diverse talents to flourish and enhances team performance.

Finally, leaders who excel in social skills are adept at managing relationships. They communicate clearly and persuasively, foster teamwork, and facilitate collective action toward shared goals. Their ability to navigate and orchestrate complex social interactions is pivotal in driving their team's success and achieving organizational objectives.

## Importance of Emotional Intelligence (EI) in Leadership

A leader skilled in emotional intelligence (EI) becomes a beacon of inspiration and motivation, crafting a work environment that is both positive and free from undue stress. This atmosphere not only uplifts the spirits but also significantly enhances productivity and performance across the board.

With a firm grasp on their emotions, such leaders are capable of making informed and impartial decisions. This ability allows them to navigate the complex waters of business challenges with clarity and strategic insight, ensuring that every choice is rooted in rational thought rather than fleeting emotion.

Furthermore, emotional intelligence endows leaders with a remarkable resilience—the capacity to bounce back swiftly from setbacks. In moments of pressure, they maintain their composure and clearheadedness, demonstrating an unshakable calm that steadies their teams.

In the intricacies of workplace dynamics, EI is instrumental in fostering deeper, more trusting relationships. It enhances collaboration, bolsters loyalty, and strengthens team cohesion, creating an environment where cooperation thrives.

Leaders who excel in emotional intelligence are particularly effective in managing the human aspects of change. They approach fears and resistance with sensitivity and tact, guiding their teams through transitions with empathy and understanding. This sensitivity ensures that changes are not only implemented but also embraced, paving the way for smoother transformations within the organization.

### Developing Emotional Intelligence in Leadership

In the realm of leadership, the cultivation of emotional intelligence is paramount. Leaders are encouraged to engage in regular self-reflection, a practice through which they can uncover the emotional triggers and patterns that shape their responses. This introspection fosters an elevated sense of self-awareness and mastery over one's emotional state.

The quest for self-improvement in leadership is further enriched by the pursuit of feedback. Constructive insights from peers, mentors, and team members serve as a mirror, reflecting the impact of a leader's emotional reactions and behaviors on others. This feedback is invaluable, as it provides a clear lens through which leaders can view and adjust their actions.

Empathy, too, is a cornerstone of effective leadership. By actively listening to and genuinely considering the perspectives of others, leaders strengthen their ability to forge meaningful connections with their teams. This empathetic approach not only aids in supporting team members but also in advocating for their needs and aspirations.

Moreover, the development of social skills plays a critical role in a leader's toolkit. Through honing their abilities in communication, conflict resolution, and relationship-building, leaders enhance their efficacy in managing the complex tapestry of interpersonal relationships.

Commitment to continuous learning is the thread that ties these elements together. By adopting a mindset geared towards ongoing personal and professional development, leaders ensure the evolution of their emotional intelligence. This continuous growth is essential not only for their personal effectiveness but also for fostering a supportive, productive, and adaptable organizational culture.

Emotional intelligence transcends the notion of a mere soft skill. It is, indeed, a vital leadership capability that supports successful team dynamics, sharpens decision-making, and bolsters organizational resilience. By placing a premium on the development of emotional intelligence, leaders not only improve their own performance but also contribute significantly to the health and prosperity of their organizations. Let's read another short story with an example:

### *A Tale of Leadership and Emotional Intelligence*

*In the heat of combat, where chaos reigns and the line between life and death blurs, Staff Sergeant Deltaco found himself not only fighting an external enemy but also navigating the tumultuous battlefield of human emotions. The principles of emotional intelligence (EI), often relegated to the boardrooms and leadership seminars, became his compass in the most unexpected of environments.*

*The realization dawned on Deltaco during a critical operation in a hostile territory. Surrounded by the loudness of gunfire and the sharp scent of fear, he observed his squad, a diverse group trained for physical endurance but not for the emotional toll of war.*

*Deltaco, a leader by rank and duty, recognized a pivotal truth: success in this operation would hinge not just on strategy and skill, but on the emotional resilience and unity of his team.*

*Self-awareness became Deltaco's first tool. Amidst the chaos, he took a moment to assess his emotions, recognizing his fear and anxiety. This awareness allowed him to address his emotions rather than let them cloud his judgment. His decisions became a reflection of strategic thought, not reactive impulse.*

*With self-regulation, he maintained his composure, setting a standard for his squad. His calm demeanor amidst the storm of conflict served as a beacon for his team, inspiring confidence, and stability.*

*Motivation was his armor! Deltaco's unwavering determination and optimistic outlook became infectious, lighting a fire within his squad that adversity could not extinguish. His belief in their mission and in everyone's capability fueled their collective drive to push forward.*

*Empathy was perhaps his most unexpected weapon. In understanding and sharing the emotions of his squad, Deltaco fostered a sense of belonging and support among the soldiers. This empathetic leadership ensured that no one felt alone in their fears or burdens, strengthening the bonds that made them not just a unit but a family.*

Did you notice how his social skills acted as the glue that held them together. Effective communication ensured clarity of orders and strategies, while his ability to resolve conflicts and encourage teamwork kept the squad focused and unified.

Under Deltaco's emotionally intelligent leadership, the squad's performance transformed. What was once a group of skilled individuals became a cohesive, resilient team. Their operations, executed with precision and unity, saw heightened success rates. Decision-making became a collective process, where diverse perspectives were valued, leading to innovative strategies and outcomes.

Their resilience soared as well. Setbacks were no longer seen as failures but as lessons. The squad's ability to bounce back from adversity with greater determination was a testament to their leader's influence.

Relationships within the squad deepened, trust flourished, and loyalty became unwavering. This transformation was not just tactical but emotional, contributing to a strengthened morale that was critical in the face of continuous adversity.

Deltaco's journey was not without its challenges. Developing his emotional intelligence required introspection and a commitment to self-improvement. He reflected on his emotional responses, seeking feedback from peers and mentors. This reflective practice helped him understand his emotional triggers and how to manage them effectively. He also committed to practicing empathy, listening actively to his squad members, and considering their perspectives. This effort deepened his understanding of his team and enhanced his ability to lead them effectively.

Deltaco recognized that developing his social skills was crucial. He worked on his communication, ensuring clarity and persuasiveness, and honed his conflict resolution skills. These efforts improved his ability to navigate complex interpersonal dynamics within his squad.

Above all, Deltaco embraced continuous learning. He sought out resources on leadership and emotional intelligence, applying new insights to his leadership approach. This commitment to growth ensured that he remained an effective leader, capable of adapting to the evolving challenges of combat and leadership.

In the crucible of combat, Staff Sergeant Deltaco discovered the profound impact of emotional intelligence on leadership and team performance. By prioritizing the development of EI competencies, he not only enhanced his effectiveness as a leader but also contributed to creating a more resilient, supportive, and successful squad. Deltaco's story is a testament to the fact that emotional intelligence is not just a soft skill but a critical capability that underpins successful leadership in any arena, even the most unexpected ones.

# 8

# Developing Leadership Presence

**Cultivating Presence and Influence**

Imagine stepping into the grand arena of leadership, where the spotlight is relentless, and the crowd is unforgiving. Here, you're not just a leader; you're the ringmaster, the showstopper, and occasionally, the janitor cleaning up the mess. This is the world where commanding presence isn't just about having the loudest voice or the biggest office, but about mastering the intricate ballet of assertiveness, charisma, and influence. It's an art, really, one that demands practice, finesse, and a good sense of humor.

The quest begins with the twin shields of confidence and assertiveness. First, confidence. It's not just about walking into a room and hoping you own it. It's about knowing you do, because you've worked hard to sharpen your skills, much like a chef perfects the art of slicing sushi—precise, deliberate, and with the right amount of flair. Building this confidence doesn't happen overnight. It's an accumulation of small victories, like successfully leading a meeting without coffee or navigating through a PowerPoint presentation without technology betraying you.

Assertiveness, on the other hand, is about clear and respectful communication. It's knowing that your voice matters and ensuring it's heard over the din. Imagine being at a bustling medieval market. You wouldn't whisper and hope to make a sale, would you? No, you'd speak clearly and directly, using "I" statements as your currency, trading passivity for participation. It's about setting boundaries too. Think of it as building a moat around your castle—not to keep everyone out, but to protect your time and energy from the dragons, otherwise known as burnout.

**The Art of Public Speaking and Presentation**

If confidence and assertiveness are your shields, then public speaking is your sword. Swinging effectively requires skill. It's about crafting messages that resonate, organizing thoughts as meticulously as a librarian sort of books, and delivering them with the ease of a seasoned storyteller. The goal is to captivate your audience, make them hang onto your every word as if you're spinning tales of heroics and adventures—not quarterly revenue forecasts.

Effective public speaking also involves engagement. Use stories, anecdotes, and even humor to breathe life into your presentations. Think of yourself as a conductor at an orchestra; every gesture, every pause, and every inflection should draw your audience in, building to a crescendo that leaves them inspired. And let's not forget about visuals—no, not the dizzying arrays of pie charts, but clear, compelling visuals that support your message like a loyal squire supports a knight.

**Crafting a Professional Image**

Now, let's talk about your armor—your professional image. This goes beyond dressing sharply or having a firm handshake (though those things certainly don't hurt). It's about aligning your external presence with your internal values. Your actions, your decisions, your interactions—they all paint a picture of who you are as a leader. Are you the villain or the hero in your story? Do you walk the talk, or do you merely talk the talk?

This image isn't just for those in your immediate orbit. Thanks to the digital age, your professional persona has the potential to travel across the internet faster than folklore. Platforms like LinkedIn are your modern-day heralds, proclaiming your achievements and expertise to the world. Ensure that these platforms reflect your professional narrative accurately and authentically, much like a bard would sing praises of your heroic deeds.

### Networking and Continuous Learning

What is a leader without their allies and confidants? Networking isn't just about collecting business cards or adding connections on social media. It's about building relationships that are as strong and reliable as a castle's foundations. And just as a castle needs regular upkeep, so too does your knowledge base. Stay abreast of industry trends, new technologies, and evolving practices. Think of it as sharpening your sword; the blade must be kept keen if it is to cut through the challenges ahead.

### Integrity and Work-Life Balance

Lastly, let us not forget the shield of integrity and the balancing act of work-life harmony. Integrity in leadership is non-negotiable. It's the trust that you foster, not just through words, but through actions consistently done right. It's your moral compass, guiding you through decisions both big and small. And as for balancing work and life, think of it as maintaining your castle's grounds—it's not just about fortifications, but also about creating spaces that allow you and those around you to thrive.

In conclusion, cultivating a leadership presence is akin to being a masterful storyteller, where your actions, words, and decisions weave together to create a compelling narrative. and lead with exemplary distinction. In the complex and ever-evolving landscape of leadership, embodying confidence and assertiveness isn't merely about directing others but about being a beacon that others are drawn to follow. This influential presence extends beyond task completion; it cultivates an environment where creativity, innovation, and collaboration thrive.

Confidence in a leader is magnetic. It attracts and retains talent, fostering a team culture where challenges are approached with a can-do attitude and failures are seen as opportunities to learn. A confident leader reassures their team, providing stability and security that empowers individuals to take risks and venture outside their comfort zones. This environment is crucial for growth and innovation, as team members feel supported in their endeavors and safe to express novel ideas.

Assertiveness, when balanced with empathy and respect, ensures that a leader's vision and objectives are clearly communicated and understood. It allows for open channels of communication where feedback is both given and received effectively. This kind of transparency in communication builds trust and respect, which are foundational to successful leadership.

Moreover, by combining these traits with strategic thinking, empathy, and adaptability, a leader doesn't just manage resources and people; they inspire loyalty and enthusiasm. Their influence encourages others to internalize the organization's goals and strive for excellence, not out of obligation, but from a genuine desire to contribute to something greater than themselves.

In addition, leaders who exhibit these qualities often serve as role models, demonstrating the behaviors and attitudes that align with the organization's values and culture. This modeling behavior is vital in shaping the organization's climate and can significantly impact its success by aligning team members with the organization's mission and values.

In sum, by embodying confidence and assertiveness alongside empathy, understanding, and adaptability, leaders do more than fulfill their roles effectively—they inspire and influence. They create a vibrant culture where members are motivated to achieve their best, paving the way for collective success and individual fulfillment. In doing so, they not only achieve their goals but also elevate the potential of their teams and the broader organization.

### *A Story of Growth and Presence*

*In the bustling world of corporate skyscrapers, where ambition collides with reality, Ethan Chambers stood as a promising yet unremarkable middle manager at Horizon Technologies. Despite his potential, Ethan's presence seemed to dissolve into the background of boardrooms and crowded hallways. Recognizing his plateau, Ethan embarked on a transformative journey to develop a commanding leadership presence, guided by the principles of confidence, assertiveness, public speaking, professional image, and continuous learning.*

*Ethan's journey began with the cornerstone of leadership: confidence. He realized that his ideas often went unheard, not because they lacked merit, but because he presented them with hesitation. Ethan committed to skill development, enrolling in workshops that sharpened his expertise in digital transformation, a critical area for Horizon Technologies. With each new competency mastered, Ethan's self-efficacy soared.*

*He adopted positive self-talk, replacing doubts with affirmations like "I am capable and insightful." Small achievements in leading project teams built his confidence, while visualization techniques prepared him mentally for challenging situations. When setbacks occurred, Ethan embraced them as learning* opportunities, understanding that each failure was a steppingstone towards resilience.

With newfound confidence, Ethan focused on cultivating assertiveness. He learned to assert his right to express his thoughts, employing "I" statements to articulate his ideas and concerns directly. Setting boundaries became crucial in maintaining his work-life balance, empowering him to say no to unreasonable demands.

Ethan rehearsed for difficult conversations, which, coupled with open body language, significantly improved his communication. This assertive approach earned him respect, allowing for more effective negotiation and conflict resolution within his team.

Recognizing the power of public speaking in leadership, Ethan sought to conquer his fear of addressing large audiences. He dedicated himself to preparation and research, tailoring his messages to resonate with his listeners. Ethan structured his presentations with clear narratives, ensuring his content was engaging and supported by compelling visuals.

To overcome nerves, he practiced relaxation techniques and familiarized himself with each venue before speaking. Through relentless practice, Ethan transformed his public speaking into a tool for inspiring action and articulating his vision for the future.

Ethan understood that a professional image was more than just dressing sharply; it was about aligning his actions with his core values and goals. He refined his wardrobe to reflect his professional identity, ensuring his appearance and conduct embodied the excellence he pursued.

He also revamped his communication skills and online presence, particularly on professional networking platforms like LinkedIn, where he shared his achievements and insights. Networking within his industry became a strategic endeavor, allowing Ethan to build valuable connections and stay abreast of emerging trends.

*Central to Ethan's leadership presence was his integrity. He prioritized honesty and reliability in all his interactions, fostering trust and transparency. Adaptability was also key, as he learned to navigate changes with grace and openness.*

*Understanding the importance of work-life balance, Ethan ensured his well-being was a priority, recognizing that his energy and focus were indispensable to his leadership effectiveness.*

*Ethan's dedication to developing his leadership presence catalyzed a remarkable transformation. From a middle manager once overshadowed by doubt, he emerged as a confident, assertive leader whose voice commanded attention and respect. He inspired his teams with clarity and vision, driving Horizon Technologies towards innovative frontiers.*

*At the annual company conference, Ethan delivered a keynote speech on the power of digital transformation, captivating his audience with his compelling narrative and authentic presence. His journey resonated with many, serving as a testament to the impact of personal growth on leadership effectiveness.*

In the end, Ethan Chambers didn't just rise within the ranks of Horizon Technologies; he elevated those around him, leaving a legacy of inspiration and proving that a true leadership presence is built on the foundation of continuous development, integrity, and the courage to embrace one's potential.

# 9

# Difference between Leadership and Management!

In the grand theater of the working world, there's an ongoing drama that confounded many—an epic saga about the battle between leadership and management. Despite the popcorn-worthy confusion, these two roles aren't just different acts in the same play: they're fundamentally distinct parts of the show, each critical to the success of any business opera.

Let's continue a little more with leadership, which could easily be the more glamorous role of the duo. Picture leaders as the charismatic conductors of an orchestra. They don't just wave their batons aimlessly but use them to inspire every section, from strings to percussion, toward producing a symphony that stirs the soul. Leaders set the stage with vision and passion, captivating their audience (or *team*) by painting a picture of what could be. They're like the dashing heroes in movies who ride into the sunset, except they're riding towards innovation and change, inspiring everyone along the way.

Then there's management, the unsung heroes of the business world. If leaders are the charismatic conductors, managers are the stagehands who make sure the lights work, the sets don't fall apart, and that everyone knows their cues. They're not about the spotlight; they're about the clipboards. Their world is one of method and order—they plan, organize, staff, direct, and control. Managers are the ones who turn the leader's broad visions into actionable, bullet-point plans. They make sure the trains run on time, that the T's are crossed, the I's dotted, and that chaos is kept at bay with the power of spreadsheets and schedules.

Now, imagine the consequences when the lines between these two get blurred. It's like putting a conductor in charge of hammering the sets or asking a stagehand to compose the music—chaos ensues, and not the fun kind. Understanding the distinction is crucial, not just for keeping the peace but for ensuring that the show goes smoothly.

Leadership is all about the "what" and "why." What are we doing? Why are we doing it? It's about setting directions, defying the status quo, and walking into the wind. Leaders are the dreamers, the big-picture thinkers who rally their troops with stirring speeches and grand visions of the future.

Management, on the other hand, is all about the "how." How do we get to where the leader wants us to go? How do we align our resources most efficiently? If leadership is about inspiring change, management is about maintaining order. It's less about walking into the wind and more about building the windmill.

Leadership thrives on change and innovation. Leaders are like gourmet chefs experimenting with new recipes, always seeking to tantalize the taste buds of their patrons. Management focuses on consistency, like fast-food franchises that keep your favorite burger tasting the same, whether you're in New York or New Delhi.

As for decision-making, leaders are like gamblers, betting big on strategies that could yield the highest rewards. They are intuitive, risk-taking, and comfortable with ambiguities. Managers are more like seasoned chess players, calculating every move, considering every risk, and meticulously planning several steps ahead.

When it comes to team interaction, leaders are motivational speakers who spark enthusiasm and drive. They are mentors, cheerleaders, and sometimes, therapists. Managers are the timekeepers, quality controllers, and sometimes, the party poopers—essential for keeping everyone in line and ensuring standards are met.

Despite these differences, the dance between leadership and management is a delicate one. Both roles are essential, and the most successful organizations know how to blend the dynamic vision of leadership with the structured practicality of management. It's about knowing when to leap forward and when to step back, when to innovate and when to adhere, when to inspire and when to enforce.

By understanding these roles better, organizations can more effectively navigate the complexities of the modern business environment. It's not about choosing leadership over management or vice versa; it's about harmonizing their strengths to create a symphony that leads to sustained organizational excellence. In the end, the magic happens when the conductor and the stagehand work in perfect harmony, each mastering their roles, yet tuned to the needs of the other, ensuring the show not only goes on but goes on spectacularly.

**Management Theories**

Now let's get into the meat and potatoes of management for a bit. Understanding the evolution of management theories is crucial for grasping the diverse approaches to effective management in various organizational contexts. This section explores the foundational theories that have shaped the management landscape, comparing their key concepts, applications, critiques, and their relevance in today's business environment.

Classical management theory emerged in the late 19th and early 20th centuries, a time of industrial revolution and organizational expansion. Pioneers like Frederick Taylor, Henri Fayol, and Max Weber laid the groundwork for what would become a blueprint for modern organizational management and structure.

Scientific Management (Taylorism): Frederick Taylor introduced scientific management, emphasizing efficiency, specialization, and a methodical approach to work to increase productivity.

Administrative Theory (Fayolism): Henri Fayol focused on management principles and functions, proposing that management could be taught and that it had universal principles applicable to every organization.

Bureaucratic Management (Weberian Bureaucracy): Max Weber's theory highlighted the importance of a hierarchical structure, detailed rules, and clear roles to achieve organization and efficiency.

These theories were revolutionary, providing a framework for the burgeoning industries of the early 20th century. Factories, governmental organizations, and later corporations applied these principles to streamline operations, enhance control, and boost productivity.

Critics argue that classical management theories often overlook the human element, treating employees more as cogs in a machine than as individuals with unique needs and potential. The rigidity and hierarchical nature of these theories can stifle creativity and flexibility, limiting responsiveness to change.

The human relations theory emerged as a response to the mechanical outlook of classical management theory, emphasizing the importance of social relations and worker satisfaction. The Hawthorne Studies, conducted by Elton Mayo and his colleagues, were pivotal in highlighting the impact of social relations on productivity.

This theory suggests that employees are motivated not just by money but by social needs and job satisfaction. It stresses the importance of management styles that consider workers' psychological and social needs.

The human relations movement led to significant changes in management practices, including the adoption of more participative decision-making processes, attention to work conditions, and the development of leadership styles that focus on human needs.

While human relations theory broadened management's focus beyond mere productivity to include employee welfare, it has been criticized for possibly manipulating workers' emotions to meet organizational goals rather than genuinely addressing their needs and well-being.

Systems theory introduces a holistic view of organizations, recognizing them as complex systems composed of interrelated parts. It emphasizes the importance of understanding the interdependencies within an organization and between the organization and its environment.

The theory distinguishes between open and closed systems, with open systems interacting with their environment. It stresses the need for adaptability and the importance of feedback loops for continuous improvement.

Systems theory has influenced organizational structure, strategic planning, and operational processes by encouraging a broader perspective that takes into account the dynamic and complex nature of organizational environments.

A common critique of systems theory is its potential for complexity and abstraction, making it challenging to apply practically in specific organizational contexts.

Contingency theory posits that there is no one-size-fits-all approach to management. Instead, the optimal course of action is contingent upon the internal and external situation facing an organization.

This theory suggests that management strategies and structures should be designed based on the specific circumstances of an organization, including its goals, environment, and technology.

Contingency theory has led to more flexible and adaptive management practices, encouraging managers to analyze their unique situations and apply management principles accordingly.

Critics of contingency theory argue that it may lack coherence and consistency, making it difficult to predict which variables are most important in any given situation.

The exploration of these management theories reveals a fascinating evolution from the rigid, hierarchical approaches of the classical era to the more human-centric and flexible frameworks of later theories. Each theory contributed unique insights into the efficient and effective management of organizations, though each also has its limitations and areas of critique.

In comparing these theories, it's evident that while classical and bureaucratic theories emphasize structure and efficiency, human relations and systems theories focus more on the people within organizations and their interrelations. Contingency theory, meanwhile, offers a more situational approach, suggesting that the effectiveness of management practices depends on specific organizational contexts.

These theories provide a valuable foundation for understanding management's complexities and the diverse strategies needed to navigate them successfully. As organizations continue to evolve, these theories' principles remain relevant, guiding managers in adapting to changing environments and leveraging human and systemic resources for organizational success.

**Historical Context and Evolution**

Leadership and management have been pivotal to the organization of work and society since ancient times, though their formal study didn't begin until the late 19th and early 20th centuries. Initially, leadership was often intertwined with one's social status or position of power, inherently linked to ruling classes or military command. In contrast, the seeds of modern management theory were sown during the Industrial Revolution, a period that demanded a shift from artisanal production to factory-based manufacturing, necessitating the organization of large groups of workers and efficient use of resources.

"The Industrial Revolution" and the subsequent rise of factories played a pivotal role in shaping the early theories of management. Figures such as Frederick Taylor (1856-1915), known as the father of scientific management, introduced principles aimed at improving labor productivity through systematic analysis and division of work. Taylor's focus on efficiency and process optimization laid the groundwork for management as a distinct function, separate from the inspirational role of a leader.

Parallelly, early leadership theories emphasized traits and behaviors that could influence and direct the masses. Great Man theories suggested that leaders were born with innate qualities that predisposed them to leadership roles, a notion that evolved into more complex understandings of leadership as researchers began to recognize the importance of situational and behavioral factors.

As the 20th century progressed, the complexity of organizational life grew, and so did the theories surround leadership and management. The Human Relations Movement, exemplified by the work of Elton Mayo in the 1920s and 1930s, highlighted the importance of social relations in the workplace, suggesting that leadership involves not only directing but also caring for employees. This era began to differentiate more clearly between the roles of leaders and managers, with leadership increasingly associated with motivating and inspiring employees, and management with organizing and coordinating their efforts.

In the latter half of the 20th century, contingency theories emerged, proposing that the effectiveness of leadership and management styles depends on the context and situation. This era saw the development of various leadership styles, such as transactional and transformational leadership, further distinguishing leadership from management by emphasizing the leader's role in inspiring change beyond mere transactional exchanges.

The digital age and globalization have further transformed the concepts of leadership and management. The rapid pace of change, the emergence of new technologies, and the increasing importance of knowledge work have emphasized the need for visionary leadership and adaptive management. Leaders are now expected to navigate complex global environments, drive innovation, and foster a culture of continuous learning. At the same time, managers are tasked with leveraging technology to optimize operations, manage diverse and dispersed teams, and ensure alignment with strategic goals.

The historical evolution of leadership and management from intertwined roles in early societies to distinct functions in modern organizations reflects the changing dynamics of work and society. While rooted in the early industrial era's emphasis on efficiency and productivity, both concepts have evolved to address the complexities of managing and leading in a globalized, fast-paced world. This historical perspective underscores the importance of both roles in achieving organizational success, each complementing the other to navigate the challenges of contemporary business landscapes.

# 10

# Functions of Management

The functions of management are fundamental to any organization, ensuring operational efficiency and strategic alignment towards achieving business objectives. Traditionally, these functions are categorized into planning, organizing, leading, and controlling, each playing a critical role in the management process.

**Planning**

Planning is the cornerstone of management functions, involving the formulation of objectives and the strategies to achieve them. This process requires a careful analysis of internal and external environments, setting realistic goals, and determining the best course of action to accomplish these goals.

- *Strategic Planning*: Involves long-term goals and strategies to achieve a competitive advantage.
- *Tactical Planning*: Focuses on the medium term, translating strategic plans into more actionable objectives.
- *Operational Planning*: Deals with the short term, detailing specific actions and resources needed to achieve tactical plans.

Planning is pivotal for organizational success, providing direction and a framework for decision-making. It involves setting priorities, allocating resources, and anticipating future challenges and opportunities.

## Organizing

Organizing involves establishing the internal organizational structure, allocating resources, and coordinating tasks to achieve the organization's objectives. This function is crucial for creating a framework within which the organization operates.

- *Designing Organizational Structure:* Defining roles, responsibilities, and hierarchical relationships to ensure efficient workflow and communication.
- *Resource Allocation*: Distributing financial, human, and material resources effectively to execute plans.
- *Process Management*: Developing and managing the processes and systems that underlie production and service delivery.
- *Application*: Effective organizing ensures that the organization's structure supports its strategy, enhances operational efficiency, and fosters flexibility and innovation.

## Controlling

Controlling involves monitoring organizational performance, comparing it with the established standards, and implementing corrective actions as necessary. This function ensures that organizational activities are aligned with the goals.

- *Performance Measurement*: Using key performance indicators (KPIs) and metrics to assess efficiency and effectiveness.

- *Feedback Mechanisms*: Implementing feedback loops to inform decision-making and promote continuous improvement.
- *Corrective Action:* Identifying deviations from plans and implementing solutions to address challenges.
- *Application*: The controlling function is essential for ensuring that the organization remains on track to achieve its objectives, allowing for adjustments in response to performance data and environmental changes.

**Integrating Functions in Practice**

In practice, these management functions are interrelated and often occur simultaneously. Effective management requires a holistic approach, integrating planning, organizing, leading, and controlling in a dynamic process that adapts to the changing needs of the organization.

- *Strategic Alignment*: Ensuring that all functions are aligned with the organization's strategic objectives.
- *Flexibility and Adaptation:* Adapting management practices to respond to internal and external changes.
- *Continuous Improvement*: Leveraging insights from the controlling function to refine planning, organizing, and leading practices.

Moving forward from the foundational aspects of management functions, we now turn our attention to management styles. This section will explore the different approaches leaders can adopt in guiding their teams and organizations, highlighting the advantages and disadvantages of each and the situational contexts in which they are most effective.

**Management Styles**

Management style refers to the way that a manager or leader interacts with staff and runs the organization or team. It encompasses how decisions are made, how authority is used, and how information is communicated. Understanding these styles is crucial for managers aiming to foster productive, positive work environments.

**Autocratic Management Style**

Autocratic management is characterized by individual control over all decisions, with little input from team members. This style is rooted in classical management theories, emphasizing efficiency and control.

- *Features*: Centralized decision-making, strict adherence to policies, and minimal employee participation.
- *Advantages:* Effective in crisis situations or when tasks require clear, direct instruction.
- *Disadvantages:* Can lead to decreased employee morale and creativity due to lack of involvement and autonomy.

**Democratic Management Style**

Democratic management, in contrast, involves sharing decision-making responsibilities with team members, valuing their input and fostering a sense of collaboration.

- *Features:* Inclusive decision-making, open communication, and encouragement of team input and feedback.
- *Advantages:* Boosts morale and job satisfaction by valuing employee contributions; encourages creativity and innovation.
- *Disadvantages*: Decision-making processes can be time-consuming, potentially delaying action.

**Laissez-Faire Management Style**

The Laissez-Faire style offers considerable autonomy to employees, with managers providing guidance and support as needed rather than directing every action.

- *Features:* High level of trust in employees, minimal direct supervision, and empowerment of team members to make decisions.
- *Advantages:* Can lead to high creativity and innovation; employees often feel highly motivated and satisfied.
- *Disadvantages:* Risk of inefficiency or lack of direction if team members are not self-motivated or clear about their objectives.

**Transformational Management Style**

Transformational leaders inspire and motivate employees to exceed their own self-interests for the good of the organization, often leading to profound changes within the organization.

- *Features:* Focus on vision, communication of high expectations, and encouragement of strong relationships.
- *Advantages:* Can lead to high levels of employee engagement and innovation; promotes a strong organizational culture.
- *Disadvantages:* May require more energy and effort from the manager; risk of burnout if expectations are too high.

**Transactional Management Style**

Transactional management relies on a system of rewards and punishments to motivate employees, focusing on achieving specific tasks and goals.

- *Features:* Clear structure, performance-based rewards, and corrective actions for underperformance.

- *Advantages:* Effective in achieving short-term goals and completing specific tasks.
- *Disadvantages:* May not encourage loyalty or creativity; overly focused on short-term achievements.

**Situational Analysis of Styles**

The effectiveness of a management style is contingent on the organizational context, including the industry, company culture, and specific team dynamics. Successful managers are often those who can adapt their style to meet the needs of their team and the situation at hand.

- *Adaptive Leadership:* The ability to switch between management styles as situations change is a valuable skill, ensuring that leaders can effectively motivate their team and achieve organizational objectives.
- *Cultural Considerations:* Organizational and national culture also play significant roles in determining the most effective management style.

Effective managers are versatile, adapting their approach to suit the needs of their team and the specific challenges they face.

**Management in Different Contexts**

The principles of management are universal, yet their application must be tailored to fit the specific needs, cultures, and objectives of different organizational types. Understanding these nuances is key to effective leadership across a diverse range of contexts.

**Corporate Management**

In the corporate world, management focuses on maximizing shareholder value, achieving competitive advantage, and ensuring long-term profitability. The dynamic and competitive nature of the corporate environment requires managers to be adept at strategic planning, financial management, and innovation.

Balancing short-term performance pressures with long-term strategic goals; navigating global competition and market volatility.

- *Adaptations:* Emphasizing strategic management, innovation, and sustainability. Corporate managers often employ a mix of management styles to motivate performance and drive growth.

**Non-Profit Organizations**

Management in non-profit organizations (NPOs) centers around achieving social, educational, or charitable objectives rather than generating profit. Leaders in NPOs must excel in resource mobilization, stakeholder engagement, and mission-driven leadership.

- *Challenges:* Limited resources, dependence on donations and grants, and the need to meet the expectations of diverse stakeholders.
- *Adaptations:* Strong focus on visionary and transformational leadership to inspire commitment to the mission. Effective NPO managers prioritize transparency, accountability, and community engagement.

**Public Sector**

Public sector management involves administering governmental organizations and agencies. It requires a unique balance of efficiency, public accountability, and service delivery, often within a politically influenced environment.

- *Challenges:* Navigating bureaucratic constraints, ensuring public accountability, and responding to political pressures.
- *Adaptations:* Public managers utilize a combination of democratic and transformational styles to foster public trust and employee engagement. They must also be adept at policy analysis and implementation.

## International Management

Managing international operations introduces complexity due to diverse cultural norms, legal systems, and market dynamics. International managers must navigate cross-cultural communication, global strategic planning, and multinational team coordination.

- *Challenges:* Cultural differences, geopolitical risks, and managing across time zones.
- *Adaptations:* A high degree of cultural intelligence and flexibility is required. Successful international managers often adopt a situational management style, adapting their approach to fit local norms and business practices.

## Challenges and Adaptations

Across all contexts, managers face the common challenge of leading their organizations through change and uncertainty. The ability to adapt management practices to the organization's specific context, culture, and challenges is a hallmark of effective leadership.

- *Innovation and Change Management:* Regardless of the context, managers must foster an environment that encourages innovation and effectively manage change.

- *Diversity and Inclusion:* Emphasizing diversity and inclusion is crucial in all organizational contexts, enhancing problem-solving, creativity, and employee satisfaction.

By adapting management practices to these specific needs, managers can lead their organizations toward achieving their objectives, whether they are profit-driven, mission-oriented, or public-serving.

## Technology and Management

The integration of technology into management practices has revolutionized the way organizations operate, communicate, and compete. From data analytics and management information systems to remote work technologies and artificial intelligence, technology offers new opportunities and challenges for managers in the digital age.

### Impact of Technology on Management Practices

Technology has dramatically altered the traditional functions of management, enabling more efficient processes, enhanced decision-making capabilities, and improved communication and collaboration across geographical boundaries.

- *Data Analytics and Decision Support:* Advanced analytics and big data technologies allow managers to glean insights from vast amounts of information, enhancing strategic planning and decision-making.
- *Automation and Efficiency:* Automation tools and software solutions streamline operational processes, reducing manual tasks and improving efficiency.
- *Remote Management and Virtual Teams:* The rise of remote work technologies has facilitated the management of distributed teams, fostering flexibility and access to global talent.

## Digital Tools and Software for Managers

A plethora of digital tools are available to assist managers in their daily tasks, ranging from project management and communication platforms to HR and finance software.

- *Project Management Tools:* Platforms like Asana, Trello, and Jira help managers organize tasks, track progress, and collaborate with team members in real-time.
- *Communication Platforms:* Tools such as Slack, Microsoft Teams, and Zoom enhance internal and external communication, supporting efficient remote work environments.
- *HR and Finance Software:* Solutions like SAP, Oracle, and Workday streamline human resources and financial management, automating payroll, recruitment, and budgeting processes.

## Remote Management and Virtual Teams

The ability to manage remote teams effectively has become increasingly important. Technology facilitates this by offering solutions for communication, collaboration, and productivity tracking.

- *Challenges:* Maintaining team cohesion, communication, and productivity in a remote setting.
- *Best Practices:* Establishing clear communication channels, fostering a culture of trust, and utilizing technology to maintain visibility into team activities and project progress.

## Future Trends

Emerging technologies such as artificial intelligence (AI), machine learning, and the Internet of Things (IoT) are poised to further transform management practices.

- *AI and Automation:* AI technologies offer potential for predictive analytics, personalized customer experiences, and automating routine management tasks.
- *IoT in the Workplace:* IoT devices can enhance operational efficiency, monitor assets, and create smarter, more connected work environments.

Technology plays a pivotal role in modern management practices, offering tools and capabilities that enhance efficiency, decision-making, and adaptability to change. Managers must stay abreast of technological trends and harness these tools effectively to lead their organizations successfully in the digital era.

Transitioning from the broad impact of technology on management, we now focus on a critical aspect that underpins the success of any organization: Human Resource Management (HRM). We will cover the strategies and practices involved in managing an organization's most valuable assets—its people.

**Human Resource Management**

Human Resource Management (HRM) encompasses a wide range of activities aimed at maximizing employee performance and ensuring that employees are able to contribute effectively to the organization's goals. HRM is not just about hiring and firing; it's about nurturing a workforce that is capable, committed, and aligned with the organizational culture and objectives.

**Recruitment and Selection**

The foundation of effective HRM lies in recruiting and selecting the right people. This process involves identifying organizational needs, attracting qualified candidates, and selecting those who are best suited to the organization's culture and objectives.

- *Strategies:* Developing clear job descriptions, utilizing various recruitment channels, and implementing rigorous selection processes.
- *Importance:* The right recruitment and selection strategies can significantly enhance organizational performance, reduce turnover, and increase employee satisfaction.

**Training and Development**

Once employees are onboard, their ongoing development becomes a key focus. Training and development programs are essential for equipping employees with the necessary skills and knowledge to perform their roles effectively and to adapt to future changes.

- *Approaches*: On-the-job training, workshops, seminars, and e-learning platforms.
- *Benefits:* Continuous development opportunities can lead to increased job satisfaction, higher productivity, and the ability to innovate and respond to change.

**Performance Management**

Performance management is a continuous process that involves setting clear expectations, monitoring performance, and providing feedback. It aims to ensure that individual and organizational objectives are aligned.

- *Components:* Goal setting, performance appraisals, and feedback mechanisms

- *Outcome:* Effective performance management helps in identifying high performers, addressing performance issues, and motivating employees towards higher achievement.

**Employee Relations**

Maintaining positive employee relations is crucial for the overall health of an organization. This involves fostering a supportive work environment, addressing grievances, and ensuring fair treatment of all employees.

- *Key Elements:* Communication, engagement initiatives, and conflict resolution mechanisms.
- *Impact:* Strong employee relations can lead to increased employee engagement, reduced absenteeism, and a more harmonious workplace.

Human Resource Management plays a central role in creating a supportive, efficient, and dynamic work environment. Through strategic recruitment, focused training and development, continuous performance management, and nurturing positive employee relations, organizations can ensure their workforce remains motivated, skilled, and aligned with their goals.

Now let's shift our focus from the internal dynamics of Human Resource Management, we now examine the broader ethical landscape within which organizations operate.

**Ethical Issues and Social Responsibility in Management**

In today's complex business environment, ethical issues and social responsibility are at the forefront of management concerns. Organizations are increasingly expected not only to pursue profitability but also to contribute positively to society and minimize their environmental footprint.

## Corporate Social Responsibility (CSR)

CSR refers to the efforts made by corporations to address their impact on society and the environment. This involves going beyond legal requirements to proactively contribute to social, environmental, and economic well-being.

- *Components:* Environmental sustainability initiatives, social equity programs, and ethical labor practices.
- *Benefits:* Enhances corporate reputation, strengthens stakeholder relationships, and can lead to competitive advantages.

## Ethical Leadership

Ethical leadership is crucial in fostering a culture of integrity and accountability within organizations. It involves leading by example, making decisions that reflect the organization's values, and ensuring ethical considerations are integral to the decision-making process.

- *Characteristics:* Transparency, fairness, and respect for individuals and the broader community.
- *Impact:* Promotes a positive organizational culture, reduces risk of ethical violations, and builds trust with employees, customers, and the public.

## Stakeholder Management

Organizations interact with a wide range of stakeholders, including employees, customers, suppliers, communities, and investors. Effective stakeholder management requires balancing diverse interests and ensuring decisions benefit not only shareholders but also other stakeholders.

- *Approaches:* Stakeholder engagement, responsive communication, and consideration of stakeholder impacts in corporate governance.
- *Outcome:* Better decision-making enhanced social license to operate, and improved long-term sustainability.

**Globalization and Ethical Challenges**

Globalization has expanded organizations' operational and ethical horizons, introducing complex ethical challenges related to cultural differences, labor practices, and environmental standards in different countries.

- *Challenges:* Navigating diverse legal and ethical standards, addressing inequality, and ensuring responsible supply chain management.
- *Strategies:* Developing global ethical guidelines, conducting due diligence in international operations, and engaging in cross-cultural ethics training.

Navigating ethical issues and embracing social responsibility are integral to contemporary management. Organizations that prioritize ethical considerations and CSR not only contribute to a better world but also build a strong foundation for long-term success. Ethical leadership, stakeholder engagement, and a commitment to social responsibility can enhance reputation, foster loyalty among employees and customers, and create sustainable competitive advantages.

Building on our comprehensive examination of management practices, the final section addresses contemporary challenges facing managers in today's rapidly evolving business landscape.

## Contemporary Challenges in Management

In an era marked by rapid technological advancement, globalization, and increasing societal expectations, managers encounter a range of challenges that require innovative solutions and adaptable leadership strategies.

### Navigating Global Crises

Global crises, such as pandemics, economic downturns, and geopolitical tensions, test the resilience and adaptability of organizations. Managers play a critical role in steering their organizations through such turbulent times.

- *Strategies:* Developing contingency plans, maintaining flexible operations, and fostering open communication with stakeholders.
- *Impact:* Effective crisis management can protect organizations from the worst impacts of global upheavals, preserving jobs and ensuring business continuity.

### Managing Diversity and Inclusion

Diversity and inclusion have become central to organizational strategies, driven by the recognition that diverse teams contribute to more innovative and effective problem-solving.

- *Approaches:* Implementing comprehensive diversity and inclusion policies, promoting cultural competency, and ensuring equitable opportunities for all employees.

- *Benefits:* Besides being a moral imperative, diversity and inclusion enhance creativity, improve employee satisfaction, and can lead to better financial performance.

## Innovation and Change Management

In the face of constant technological changes and competitive pressures, fostering a culture of innovation and effectively managing change are essential for organizational survival and growth.

- *Challenges:* Overcoming resistance to change, staying ahead of technological advancements, and continually adapting business models.
- *Best Practices:* Encouraging a culture of learning and experimentation, engaging employees in the change process, and leveraging technology to drive innovation.

## Environmental Sustainability

Environmental sustainability has emerged as a critical issue for organizations, with stakeholders increasingly demanding responsible environmental practices.

- *Initiatives:* Reducing carbon footprints, implementing sustainable supply chain practices, and investing in green technologies.
- *Advantages:* Sustainable practices not only mitigate environmental impact but also can lead to cost savings, enhanced brand reputation, and compliance with regulatory requirements.

Contemporary managers face a landscape marked by challenges that are as diverse as they are complex. Successful navigation of these challenges requires a blend of strategic foresight, ethical leadership, and a commitment to innovation and sustainability. By addressing these issues proactively, managers can lead their organizations toward long-term success and make a positive impact on society and the environment.

Leadership and management are two distinct facets of organizational success, each playing a crucial role but differing fundamentally in approaches, objectives, and outcomes.

Leadership is primarily about setting a vision, inspiring, and motivating people to reach common goals. Leaders focus on influencing, guiding in the direction of the vision, and empowering individuals by fostering innovation, creativity, and personal growth. They thrive on change, looking for opportunities to innovate and move forward.

Management, on the other hand, concentrates on establishing, maintaining, and optimizing the organizational processes and systems to achieve the set objectives efficiently and effectively. Managers aim to bring order and consistency by planning, organizing, directing, and controlling resources, including personnel, finances, and assets. They work within established structures to ensure stability and predictability.

# The Key differences and a Thanks

### Vision vs. Execution

Leaders create and sell the vision, while managers are the ones who take that vision and break it down into actionable steps.

### Change vs. Stability

Leadership is about driving change and moving forward, whereas management seeks to maintain stability and control.

### Empowering vs. Directing

Leaders empower others to achieve the vision, while managers direct efforts and resources to ensure tasks are completed.

In closing, I want to emphasize that while leadership and management have their unique roles, both are indispensably vital for the thriving of any organization. To navigate the ever-evolving complexities of modern business landscapes, a harmonious blend of visionary leadership and meticulous management is crucial. Achieving this synergy is not merely beneficial—it's essential for sustained success.

I am profoundly grateful that you chose to spend your time with my book. My sincerest hope is that the insights shared here will resonate with you and find practical application in your approach to leadership. Every concept discussed, beyond the narratives shared, has been rigorously researched and grounded in years of real-world application and continuous learning. The journey of leadership is perpetually unfolding, constantly inviting us to grow, adapt, and improve.

Throughout my career, I have found that transparency, compassion, motivation, and honesty are not just principles, but powerful tools that have greatly contributed to my success. By embracing these values, I believe you can also enhance your effectiveness and influence as a leader.

Thank you once again for joining me on this journey through the pages of this book. It is my fervent hope that you will carry forward these lessons, integrating them into your leadership style, and that they will serve you as well as they have served me. Together, let us continue to learn, inspire, and lead with integrity and passion.

Shawn Eaton was raised in Clarksville, Arkansas, where he graduated from Clarksville High School in 1996. In 1997, he joined the US Army and

embarked on a distinguished 20-year military career, culminating in his retirement as a Senior Noncommissioned Officer on June 30, 2017.

During his time in the Army, Shawn deployed to combat zones four times, twice each to Iraq and Afghanistan, serving as a Staff Sergeant, Sergeant First

Class, and First Sergeant. His exemplary service earned him numerous awards, including three Bronze Stars, five Army Commendations Medals, and five
Army Achievement Medals.

He graduated from Central Texas College and completed multiple Noncommissioned Officer (NCO) courses at the NCO Academy, focusing on

leadership and leadership development.

Shawn is a proud father of five children and grandfather of four grandchildren. He has been married to his beautiful wife, Randi, for 18 years.

# *Bibliography*

Lencioni, Patrick. *"The Five Dysfunctions of a Team: A Leadership Fable"*. Jossey-Bass, 2002.

Goleman, Daniel, Richard Boyatzis, and Annie McKee. *"Primal Leadership: Learning to Lead with Emotional Intelligence"*. Harvard Business School Press, 2002.

Tuckman, Bruce W. "Developmental Sequence in Small Groups." *"Psychological Bulletin"*, vol. 63, no. 6, 1965, pp. 384–399.

Northouse, Peter. *"Leadership: Theory and Practice"*. 8th ed., 2021.

Maxwell, John C. *"Developing the Leader Within You"*. 1993.

George, Michael L., et al. *"The Lean Six Sigma Pocket Toolbook: A Quick Reference Guide to Nearly 100 Tools for Improving Quality and Speed"*. McGraw-Hill Education.

Dweck, Carol S. *"Mindset: The New Psychology of Success"*. Ballantine Books.

Taleb, Nassim Nicholas. *"Antifragile: Things That Gain from Disorder"*. Random House, 2012.

Kahneman, Daniel, and Amos Tversky. *"Thinking, Fast and Slow"*. Farrar, Straus and Giroux, 2011.

Pritchard, Carl L. *"Risk Management: Concepts and Guidance"*. 5th ed., ESI International, 2014.

Knight, Frank. *"Risk, Uncertainty, and Profit"*. Houghton Mifflin, 1921.

Edmondson, Amy. *"The Fearless Organization"*. Wiley, 2019.

# Bibliography

Amabile, Teresa M., and Mukti Khaire. "*Creativity and the Role of the Leader.*" Harvard Business Review, October 2008.

Tetlock, Philip E., and Dan Gardner. "*Superforecasting: The Art and Science of Prediction.* Random House, 2015.

Goleman, Daniel. "*Emotional Intelligence: Why It Can Matter More Than IQ*". Bantam Books, 1995.

Kotter, John P. "*Leading Change*". Harvard Business School Press, 1996.

Lewin, Kurt. "*Field Theory in Social Science*". Harper & Brothers, 1951.

Hiatt, Jeff. "*ADKAR: A Model for Change in Business, Government and our Community*". Prosci Learning Center Publications, 2006.

Peters, Thomas J., and Robert H. Waterman. "*In Search of Excellence*". Harper & Row, 1982.

Bridges, William. "*Managing Transitions: Making the Most of Change*". 3rd ed., Da Capo Press, 2009.

Kotter, John P., and Leonard A. Schlesinger. "*Choosing Strategies for Change.*" Harvard Business Review, July-August 1979.

Kotter, John P. "*Leading Change: Why Transformation Efforts Fail.*" Harvard Business Review, March-April 1995.

Schein, Edgar H. "*Organizational Culture and Leadership*". 4th ed., Jossey-Bass, 2010.

Fisher, Roger, and William Ury. "*Getting to Yes: Negotiating Agreement Without Giving In*". Penguin Books, 2011.

Pink, Daniel H. "*Drive: The Surprising Truth About What Motivates Us*". Riverhead Books, 2009.

Sinek, Simon. "*Leaders Eat Last: Why Some Teams Pull Together and Others Don't*". Portfolio, 2014.

Kouzes, James M., and Barry Z. Posner. "*The Leadership Challenge: How to Make Extraordinary Things Happen in Organizations.* 6th ed., Jossey-Bass, 2017.

Brown, Brené. *"Daring Greatly: How the Courage to Be Vulnerable Transforms the Way We Live, Love, Parent, and Lead"*. Gotham Books, 2012.

Collins, Jim. *"Good to Great: Why Some Companies Make the Leap...and Others Don't"*. HarperBusiness, 2001.

Lucas, Stephen E. *"The Art of Public Speaking"*. 13th ed., McGraw-Hill Education, 2020.

Anderson, Chris. *"TED Talks: The Official TED Guide to Public Speaking"*. Houghton Mifflin Harcourt, 2016.

Berkun, Scott. *"Confessions of a Public Speaker"*. O'Reilly Media, 2010.

Reynolds, Garr. *"Presentation Zen: Simple Ideas on Presentation Design and Delivery"*. 2nd ed., New Riders, 2012.

Donovan, Jeremey. *"How to Deliver a TED Talk: Secrets of the World's Most Inspiring Presentations"*. McGraw-Hill Education, 2013.

Clark, Dorie. *"Reinventing You: Define Your Brand, Imagine Your Future"*. Harvard Business Review Press, 2013.

www.ingramcontent.com/pod-product-compliance
Lightning Source LLC
LaVergne TN
LVHW010550070526
838199LV00063BA/4924